TEACHINGS OF THE BIBLE

THE TRUE LIGHT

LESLIE M. JOHN

TEACHINGS OF THE BIBLE

THE TRUE LIGHT

LESLIE M. JOHN

The entire text of this book and graphics are deposited with Library of Congress Copyright Office, 101 Independence Avenue, SE Washington, DC 20559-6000, USA. This work is protected by Law in US and internationally, according to The Berne Convention 1971

Description:

Lord Jesus Christ is the true light. He is the Son of God, the very God Himself. His teachings give us great insight into our sinful life on this earth and joyful life in eternity.

Apostle John explains that the true Light, which lights every man born into this world, was Lord Jesus Christ. He came into the world, which He made, and lived among men, but the world did not know Him, nor did the world perceive who He was. He came unto His own, and His own did not receive Him.

The Lord gave the privilege to become the sons of God to all those who believed Him, even to them that believed on His name, and were born of God; not of flesh and blood, or of the desires of the flesh.   The Word became incarnate God and lived among us and He was Lord Jesus Christ.

"That was the true Light, which lighteth every man that cometh into the world. He was in the world, and the world was made by him, and the world knew him not. He came unto his own, and his own received him not. But as many as received him, to them gave he power to become the sons of God, even to them that believe on his name: Which were born, not of blood, nor of the will of the flesh, nor of the will of man, but of God. And the Word was made flesh, and dwelt among us, (and we beheld his glory, the glory as of the only begotten of the Father,) full of grace and truth" (John 1:9-14).

ISBN-13: 978-0-9985181-0-7

ISBN-10: 0-9985181-0-7

TABLE OF CONTENTS

PREFACE

For God so loved the world, that he gave his only begotten Son, that whosoever believeth in him should not perish, but have everlasting life. For God sent not his Son into the world to condemn the world; but that the world through him might be saved. (John 3:16-17)

Lord Jesus Christ is the Son of God and He said He and the Father are one. No one comes to Him unless the Father draws one to the Lord. Jesus Christ is the creator and not a created being. He is superior to the entire creation.

"For by him were all things created, that are in heaven, and that are in earth, visible and invisible, whether they be thrones, or dominions, or principalities, or powers: all things were created by him, and for him: And he is before all things, and by him all things consist. And he is the head of the body, the church: who is the beginning, the firstborn from the dead; that in all things he might have the preeminence" (Colossians 1:16-18)

This book presents sublime theme of man's redemption from sin and everlasting life. Man rebelled against God by transgressing His command.

The only way available for reconciling man with God was by the substitutionary death of the Lord Jesus Christ and by His resurrection. Whoever believes in Him will not perish but will have everlasting life.

Bible says: "For all have sinned, and come short of the glory of God" (Romans 3:23)

"For the wages of sin is death; but the gift of God is eternal life through Jesus Christ our Lord" (Romans 6:23)

"If we say that we have no sin, we deceive ourselves, and the truth is not in us" (1 John 1:8)

"That if thou shalt confess with thy mouth the Lord Jesus, and shalt believe in thine heart that God hath raised him from the dead, thou shalt be saved. For with the heart man believeth unto righteousness; and with the mouth confession is made unto salvation" (Romans 10:9-10)

CHAPTER 1
LIGHT OF THE WORLD

"Then spake Jesus again unto them, saying, I am the light of the world: he that followeth me shall not walk in darkness, but shall have the light of life" (John 8:12)

There were, in this world, many who taught that we should do good works and live holy life, but none could practically redeem any man from sin, when a man fails to keep meticulously the commandments and statutes of God.

There is no one who can claim that he/she is perfect in all respects in this world. What then is the remedy to get out of sin and receive salvation? Is it by doing some more good works that we receive salvation?

When we weigh in balance our good works and bad works that we do in our day-to-day life, we are sure to observe that our bad works outweigh always the good works that we do. After all we are made out of dust and will return to dust. That is why the grace of God is needed to get out of the clutches of this dark world that we live in. The only one who can get us out from that miry clay of sin, is the one who offered Himself as sacrifice and shed His blood for our sake, and He is the Lord Jesus Christ, and He alone is the light of the world.

It can, therefore, be said without any reluctance that there is no one, except Lord Jesus Christ, who can claim that he/she is the light of the world. The Lord not only claimed that He is the light of the world but He also said that whoever follows him shall not walk in darkness, but will have the light of life.

If we look into the claim He made we can see that there is none who came down from heaven leaving behind the glory that He had with the Father in heaven, and taking the likeness of man to live among earth-dwellers like a man in flesh, and sacrifice His life for the sake of us, the earth-dwellers.

We are made of dust and are worth nothing but to be cast into eternal fire for the transgression we did of the commandment of God. The first man on this earth was on probation to prove his worth to walk with God as His friend. He enjoyed the fellowship in the cool of the day with the Almighty God, but he transgressed the commandment of the Lord. God said that he should not eat of the fruit of the tree that was in the middle of the Garden of Eden, where he was placed to enjoy the light from the LORD. However, the man proved that he was fallible and was indeed a mere man, and eventually fell into darkness. We all carry Adam's sin in our DNA, and unless that sin is covered and washed by the Lord, we cannot see the kingdom of God.

God created man in His own image and took one of his ribs and made out of it a woman and gave her to him as his wife. The first man, Adam called her "bone of my bones, and flesh of my flesh" (Ref. Gen. 2:23) She listened to the commandment of God while she was in the man, and yet she was the first one to yield to the temptation of the serpent, which was more subtle than any of the beasts of the field that the LORD God had made.

The small world where they enjoyed the presence of heavenly light was soon gone, and they found themselves naked. They hid themselves from the presence of God wearing a temporary apron that they made from the fig leaves to cover their nakedness. God created them naked and He knew their nakedness, and yet they realized that they were naked only after they transgressed the commandment of the LORD. God made clothing for them from the skin of the slain animal and put on them that robe, and chased them out from the Garden of Eden into this dark world.

Ever since they were out into this dark world they struggled to be out from the darkness, and the only possibility was to have God as their rock of refuge and light. Their redemption from sin was possible only if they were covered by the blood of animal.

However, it was temporary covering, and the permanent covering was to come much later into this world in the form of the blood of Lord Jesus Christ. There is no remission of sin unless the sin of man is cleansed in the blood of Lord Jesus Christ, who was crucified on the cross and died on behalf of us, and was buried and later raised by God on the third day from the dead.

Until Lord Jesus came into this world as incarnate God, the LORD provided a temporary resolution for the people of Old Testament to sacrifice animals on the altar that their sins may be covered. Jesus came into this world as incarnate God, in due time, and while we were yet sinners, He died for all men, and thus animals sacrifices were done away with. Whoever confesses Him as the Lord and Savior and believes that God raised Him from the dead will receive that eternal light, which is of the Lord alone.

In Revelation 1:13-18 the description of Lord Jesus Christ is given. He was in the midst of the seven lampstands, "clothed with a long robe and with a golden sash around his chest. The hairs of his head were white, like white wool, like snow. His eyes were like a flame of fire, his feet were like burnished bronze, refined in a furnace, and his voice was like the roar of many waters. In his right hand he held seven stars, from his mouth came a sharp two-edged sword, and his face was like the sun shining in full strength"

The types and shadows were shown in the Old Testament period. God said to Moses that there should be seven lamps on a lampstand, which is also called "Menorah" in the Tabernacle, and the children of Israel were commanded that they should fill the lamps with pure olive oil to cause the lamp to burn continuously. (cf. Exo. 25:37; 27:20)

When John saw in his vision, Lord Jesus Christ, he fell at the Lord's feet as though he were dead, but the Lord laid His right hand on Him saying "Fear not, I am the first and the last, and the living one. I died, and behold I am alive forevermore, and I have the keys of Death and Hades" (Read... Revelation 1:13-18 ESV)

Lord Jesus Christ was in the form of God and yet He preferred to take the form a servant and the likeness of man and humbled Himself by becoming obedient to die on the cross for our sake. (cf. Philippians 2:6-11)

The Lord gave us that light and made us burning lamps to reflect His light in this world in order that we may glorify the name of the Father in heaven. He said we are the light of the world, and that we should shine before men that the world may see the Lord's attributes in us. Lord Jesus Christ is the light of the world.

It is evident, therefore, that we are saved by His grace and we reflect His light and do good works; but our salvation is not by good works, but by the grace of God by faith in Him.

CHAPTER 2
EVENING AND DAY

And God saw the light, that it was good: and God divided the light from the darkness. And God called the light Day, and the darkness he called Night. And the evening and the morning were the first day. (Genesis 1:4-5)

There was darkness and God said let there be light and there was light. God divided darkness and light. It should be noted that there was darkness first and then came the light when God called it to be there. When the light came the darkness disappeared. First it was evening, and then the morning, and that is why we read that the evening and the day together was called the first day in Genesis 1:5. Then, God placed Sun and Moon in the firmament in order to distinguish between seasons, and times.

Similarly, when Lord Jesus Christ, who is Light and the Truth, came into the world, the darkness and falsehood disappeared from those who believed Him as Savior. However, the darkness in the hearts of those who did not believe Him as Savior was still there. This darkness did not comprehend the Light.

And the light shineth in darkness; and the darkness comprehended it not. (John 1:5)

When the Light is covered partially with a shade there is hazy light all over except where the rays of light directly fall. There is perfect light on regions where the light falls. The covering of the light in this case was deliberate and done on purpose; otherwise the light would be all over the regions where the power of the light penetrates.

The earth has light and darkness simultaneously in different regions, but where there is darkness, it is partial with moon and stars still ruling the partial darkness. The subterranean region of the earth has absolutely no light because the light does not penetrate into that region. It is at that place that there is total darkness.

Many people prefer to remain in partially covered regions where the power of the light is obliterated deliberately; otherwise, there is no power to stop the powerful light from Lord Jesus Christ. The only region where there is total darkness is under the earth, and it is subterranean region, which is the kingdom of devil.

And this is the condemnation, that light is come into the world, and men loved darkness rather than light, because their deeds were evil. (John 3:19)

Man is made out of dust, and he will return to dust when he dies, but the soul of man never dies. The spirit of man, whether saved or not will go to back to God, who blew into man's nostrils the breath of life, when he created him. The soul without spirit is not live, and will remain in a region allotted by God. The place is either of comfort or condemnation, until they are fully made alive; righteous to live with God and the unrighteous to be cast into the 'lake of fire'. Those are the two resurrections. The saved will rise to be with the Lord forever, while the unsaved will be cast into the 'lake of fire'.

The souls of the saved ones are led to the perfect Light where Lord Jesus Christ is the Light. There is no sun or moon to give light in eternity. The present creation, the heaven and the earth will pass away; "the elements shall melt with fervent heat" and will be in the holy city, New Jerusalem coming down from God out of heaven, prepared as a bride for her husband.(cf. Matt. 24:35; 2 Peter 3:10; Isaiah 35:17; Rev. 21:1)

Then spake Jesus again unto them, saying, I am the light of the world: he that followeth me shall not walk in darkness, but shall have the light of life. (John 8:12)

Then Jesus said unto them, Yet a little while is the light with you. Walk while ye have the light, lest darkness come upon you: for he that walketh in darkness knoweth not whither he goeth. (John 12:35)

I am come a light into the world, that whosoever believeth on me should not abide in darkness. (John 12:46)

CHAPTER 3
THE TRUE LIGHT

In the beginning God created the heaven and the earth. And the earth was without form, and void; and darkness was upon the face of the deep. And the Spirit of God moved upon the face of the waters. And God said, Let there be light: and there was light. (Genesis 1:1-3)

Creation started at some point of time, and God was there to create, and He was "In the beginning". Unless He was there before the creation began, He could not be the creator. Therefore, there was a time when God called creation into existence, and that was the 'beginning'; beginning of what? It was not the beginning of God, but it is beginning of the God's creation. God is outside time. Job says..

"Behold, God is great, and we know him not, neither can the number of his years be searched out". (Job 36:26)

Apostle John rightly said that 'without him was not anything made that was made '

"All things were made by him; and without him was not anything made that was made". (John 1:3)

God started creating this universe and everything in it, as some point of time, and that point of time is, as Scriptures call it, as "In the beginning". The point of time when God started His creation is not a measurement of time according to eternal God. The LORD specified the measurement of time, and He did it as recorded in Genesis 1:5.

"And God called the light Day, and the darkness he called Night. And the evening and the morning were the first day" (Genesis 1:5)

God is always in the present tense. It is for the purpose of understanding of man that, in the limitation of expression of language, it is written as "In the beginning". The fact that the earth was without form and void should not render misinterpretation of Scriptures that Satan violently interfered in the creation of God. This is an assumption made by some as a result of unbelief in the Almighty power of God. This assumption has no scriptural support.

All that the phrase "And the earth was without form, and void" means that the earth was empty and wasteful before the LORD created plants, animals etc. "Darkness was upon the face of the deep, and the Spirit of God moved upon the face of the waters".

The creation was in progress and, therefore, Genesis 1:5b reads..." And the evening and the morning were the first day". The creation from the start until the end of the first day consisted of the creation of 'the heaven', creation of 'the earth'; calling the light into existence, dividing the light and the darkness and calling the light as "Day" and the darkness as the "Night".

"And God said, Let there be light: and there was light. And God saw the light, that it was good: and God divided the light from the darkness. And God called the light Day, and the darkness he called Night. And the evening and the morning were the first day" (Genesis 1:3-5)

It is very important to note that God saw that the light was good, and therefore, He divided the light from the darkness.

Darkness flees away when the light shines. One small ray of light is enough to dispel the effect of darkness, but darkness cannot dispel the light.

Apostle John wants us to understand the very touching point that in Lord Jesus was life, and that life was the light of men. When light shone in darkness, the darkness comprehended it not.

"In him was life; and the life was the light of men. And the light shineth in darkness; and the darkness comprehended it not" (John 1:4-5)

John, the Baptist, (not the Apostle John, who was a disciple of Lord Jesus), was a forerunner of Lord Jesus. He was the voice in the wilderness crying "... Prepare ye the way of the Lord, make his paths straight" John the Baptist did baptize in the wilderness, and preached the baptism of repentance for the remission of sins. Many from the land of Judaea, and from Jerusalem that confessed their sins, were baptized of him in the river of Jordan. (cf. Mark 1:3-5)

John the Baptist was a witness who bore witness of the Light that all men might believe in Lord Jesus. He cleared their speculations that he was perhaps the Christ or Elias, inasmuch as he was baptizing. However, he said he baptized with water, but referring to Lord Jesus, who was standing among them, that Lord Jesus was preferred before him, and he was not worthy to unloose latchet of the Lord's shoe.

John the Baptist said that he was not that Light, but pointing to Lord Jesus he said he came to bear witness of the True Light, who was Lord Jesus Christ, who gives Light to every man coming into this world (ref. John 1:6-9)

CHAPTER 4
THE TRUE LIGHT - Part II

"That was the true Light, which lighteth every man that cometh into the world. He was in the world, and the world was made by him, and the world knew him not. He came unto his own, and his own received him not. But as many as received him, to them gave he power to become the sons of God, even to them that believe on his name: Which were born, not of blood, nor of the will of the flesh, nor of the will of man, but of God. And the Word was made flesh, and dwelt among us, (and we beheld his glory, the glory as of the only begotten of the Father,) full of grace and truth" (John 1:9-14).

Apostle John explains that the true Light, which lights every man born into this world, was Lord Jesus Christ. He came into the world, which He made, and lived among men, but the world did not know Him, nor did the world perceive who He was. He came unto His own, and His own did not receive Him.

The Lord gave the privilege to become the sons of God to all those who believed Him, even to them that believed on His name, and were born of God; not of flesh and blood, or of the desires of the flesh. The Word became incarnate God and lived among us and He was Lord Jesus Christ.

Apostle John and other disciples saw His glory, the glory of the only Son of the Father, and He was full of grace and truth. The Lord was exact representation of the Father, and He and the Father were and are one.

God created Heaven first and then the earth; however the earth did not appear above the waters, which were covered with thick darkness and the Spirit of God moved upon its surface. It was then that God commanded that there should be light, and the light came into existence. The LORD divided Light from the darkness. He called the Light as DAY and the darkness as NIGHT. Evening and the morning was the FIRST DAY.

God placed heaven over the whole creation that He would create by which we know that it was God's desire that heaven should stand by itself and be above all other creation. He placed a firmament, which was crystalline (a transparent formation) firmament around it in such a manner that it fits around the earth and gives moisture and rain. God was continuously at work for six days and He rested on the seventh day.

Let us think of a man who, while assembling a machine, would need a part from another source, before he completes the first part; in which case he would keep aside the first part and would gather the second part and puts it into the first part and completes the work one after another.

Similarly, God would have left earth under water for another day until he finished the work on heaven and the firmament, before He allowed earth to appear on the surface of the waters. In any case the earth was never under water beyond the third day.

God commanded the dry land to appear with seas around it. He commanded earth to bring forth grass, herb yielding seed, and fruit after its kind, whose seed in itself upon the earth, after its kind. And the evening and the morning were the third day.

The Sun was not the source of light but the two great lights were made to rule the DAY and the NIGHT respectively. When God commanded the Light to come into existence on the very first day of His creation, the Light came into existence, and when the light came into existence, Sun and Moon were not there. Sun and Moon came into existence on the fourth day of God's creation.

God divided Light from the darkness. God made stars also. When God made two great lights he did not call them Sun and Moon; however, many chapters later in Genesis 15:12 and 17; 37:9 these terms were used. Sun was to rule the DAY and the Moon was to rule the NIGHT. God set the two great lights in the firmament.

God said let the lights be in the firmament of the heaven to give light upon the earth and to divide the Day from the NIGHT, and "let them be for signs, and for seasons, and for days, and years". This is how the time started. The two great lights were made to distinguish between seasons, days and years. And the evening and the morning were the fourth day.

CHAPTER 5
THE TRUE LIGHT – Part III

"The next day John seeth Jesus coming unto him, and saith, Behold the Lamb of God, which taketh away the sin of the world" (John 1:29).

While John the Baptist was baptizing in water Jews sent priests and Levites from Jerusalem to inquire as to who he was. John the Baptist said He was neither Christ nor Elias or prophet, but he was the forerunner of Lord Jesus Christ. Next day when he saw Lord Jesus coming to him, he proclaimed that the Lord was the "Lamb of God", who takes away the sin of the world.

Clearly John the Baptist was pointing to the Old Testament substitutionary sacrifices of animals that were offered, in order to cleanse the sins of each one, who confessed his sin by placing his hands on the lamb's head, in the presence of priest. It is pathetic that in the present age, many Jews do not believe that substitutionary death of a savior is necessary to cleanse their sin, even though they believe that substitutionary offering of sacrifice was necessary as recorded in the Old Testament for the remission of sins. It is hard for them to acknowledge that everyone is sinner by birth and except by accepting that Savior's death on behalf sinner was necessary for the remission of sins. They believed that Messiah will be born in a palace like a princess and he would defeat their enemies like a king.

There will come surely a time when the Lord will come again and defeat their enemies and His enemies. The time is not far away. Everything is happening in God's time. In due time,

Christ died for us. In due time He will make the Jews and all others acknowledge that He is the Lord and except by acknowledging Him as the Savior, there is no salvation.

John the Baptist said it was Lord Jesus, the "Lamb of God" about whom he said that even though he was born before the Lord was born on this earth, the Lord was already there and He is eternal. He said he was baptizing with water in order that the Lord should be made manifest to Israel. As Lord Jesus was coming to him, he reiterated saying "Behold the Lamb of God!"

"And looking upon Jesus as he walked, he saith, Behold the Lamb of God!" (John 1:36).

John the Baptist was reluctant to baptize Lord Jesus, who came from Galilee to Jordan to be baptized of him; but the Lord said to him "Suffer it be now" indicating that it was required to fulfill all righteousness. Then John the Baptist baptized Lord Jesus.

While Lord Jesus was coming out of the water, "the heavens were opened unto him, and he saw the Spirit of God descending like a dove, and lighting upon him: And lo a voice from heaven, saying, this is my beloved Son, in whom I am well pleased" (cf. Matthew 3:13-17). Here is the endorsement from the Father that Jesus was the Son of God. Likewise, after Jesus died, and was raised from the dead, the Father acknowledged the Son as God, equal with Him, and yet He gave all the power to Him (cf. Matthew 28:18)

"But unto the Son he saith, Thy throne, O God, is for ever and ever: a sceptre of righteousness is the sceptre of thy kingdom" (Hebrews 1:8)

Old Testament prophecy is fulfilled...

"Thy throne, O God, is for ever and ever: the sceptre of thy kingdom is a right sceptre" (Psalms 45:6).

Lord Jesus is the "Word', who was with God, and the Word was God", and "And the Word was made flesh, and dwelt among us" (cf. John 1:1, 14). He is the Christ, i.e. He is the Messiah.

When there was total darkness and the Spirit of God was hovering upon the deep waters, God said let there be light be and there was light. When the light came into existence the darkness was dispelled. When Adam was with God in fellowship with Him, they communed with each other freely, but when the man sinned against God he lost the image of God, and darkness engulfed him. Adam walked in the light, he was in the light until he committed sin and was thrown out of the Garden of Eden.

Here is the True light, Lord Jesus Christ, who came in the likeness of man, to offer Himself as sacrifice on behalf of us. There is a provision made for man to accept that light, and be saved. He is the Way, the Truth and the Life. Whoever accepted the Light had no darkness in him.

Lord Jesus Christ is the Light in eternity, where there will be no Sun, or moon.

CHAPTER 6
THE TRUE LIGHT – PART IV

Now is my soul troubled; and what shall I say? Father, save me from this hour: but for this cause came I unto this hour. Father, glorify thy name. Then came there a voice from heaven, saying, I have both glorified it, and will glorify it again. (John 12:27-28)

People heard a voice from heaven saying "I have glorified it, and I will glorify again" in response to Lord Jesus prayer to the Father asking if He should say that the suffering He was going to endure should be removed from Him; nay but the Lord immediately says to the Father that He came to die on behalf of men. The people thought an angel spoke to the Lord; but it was the voice was from heaven for the people that the Father had glorified the Son's death, His burial and resurrection.

Lord Jesus said to them that the judgment of this word is near. The ruler of this world will be cast out when He is lifted up on the cross, and thereafter He will draw people unto Himself. In saying these words Lord Jesus was saying to them the terrible suffering that He has to endure on the cross, on their behalf. He said earlier in John 3:14 that just as Moses lifted up the brazen serpent in the wilderness, He, as a "Son of man" was to be lifted up. (cf. Numbers 21:9; John 3:14; John 6:44)

"Then said Jesus unto them, When ye have lifted up the Son of man, then shall ye know that I am he, and that I do nothing of myself; but as my Father hath taught me, I speak these things" (John 8:28).

The crowd questioned the Lord as to who the "Son of man" is that He should be lifted up and die for them. Their question was based on their belief that Messiah would never die and will rule forever according to Scriptures such as Psalm 110:4; Daniel 2:44; 8:13-14; Isaiah 9:7.

However, they never gave credence to the Scriptures from Isaiah 53:1-12. If they believed that Scriptures from Isaiah 53:1-12 were prophecy of the Lord's suffering, death, and Psalm 16:10, and Psalms 22:19-21 of His resurrection, they would not have had such rejection of Lord Jesus Christ as their Messiah as Pharisees did then, and many Jews do now. Salvation is available for everyone who confesses Jesus as Lord and believes in His death, burial and resurrection. He was divine, and yet He came down from heaven into this world in the likeness of man, and in suffering He took the nature of man.

"For thou wilt not leave my soul in hell; neither wilt thou suffer thine Holy One to see corruption" (Psalms 16:10).

"Whom God hath raised up, having loosed the pains of death: because it was not possible that he should be holden of it" (Acts 2:24).

"God hath fulfilled the same unto us their children, in that he hath raised up Jesus again; as it is also written in the second psalm, Thou art my Son, this day have I begotten thee. And as concerning that he raised him up from the dead, now no more to return to corruption, he said on this wise, I will give you the sure mercies of David. Wherefore he saith also in another psalm, Thou shalt not suffer thine Holy One to see corruption" (Acts 13:33-35)

Daniel 12:2 also speaks of resurrection of souls in general some to everlasting life, and some to shame and everlasting contempt.

"And many of them that sleep in the dust of the earth shall awake, some to everlasting life, and some to shame and everlasting contempt" (Daniel 12:2)

Therefore, Lord Jesus said to them that He was the true light and that light will be with them for a little while more; and warned them to believe on Him, while He was there in the world. He is the true light and they should believe in Him that they may become "sons of light". He said to them that they would grope in darkness if they do not walk in His light.

Everyone should seek to understand what the true light is, and follow the Lord in His light, rather than groping in darkness and head to an unknown destination.

Paul writes in Romans 11:1-36 that God did not cast away the children of Israel, but they are blinded for a season until the fullness of Gentiles is come in. What a great privilege is that Gentiles are able to come to the Lord now.

"For I would not, brethren, that ye should be ignorant of this mystery, lest ye should be wise in your own conceits; that blindness in part is happened to Israel, until the fulness of the Gentiles be come in" (Romans 11:25)

Lord Jesus warned them that if His words are of everlasting life and if His words are rejected they will be judged (cf. John 12:48-50). Does it scare that after the final great white throne judgment the unbeliever's soul will be cast into the 'lake of fire', where there is no end for gnashing of teeth, nor does the fire quench.

Highly exalted is the LORD God Almighty. He deserves to be worshipped by everyone because He is the creator of all and everything. He had all the glory in heaven with the Father and yet He relinquished His glory and came down in the form of a servant and in the likeness of man to save sinners.

Alas! Even though Lord Jesus did many miracles before the Jewish crowd, and spoke to them the truth about Him that He was sent by the Father to speak the words of the Father, yet they did not believe in Him. Lord Jesus quoted prophecies from Isaiah 51:9; 52:10; 53:1-3 and said to them they did not believe on Him and that their eyes are blinded, and their hearts are hardened (cf. John 12:37-41). Their hardening of their hearts was like Pharaoh who hardened his heart. It is because Pharaoh repeatedly hardened his heart, God hardened his heart further that the LORD may be glorified by rescuing the children of Israel from the bondage of slavery with His strong arm (cf. Exo. 6:6; Deut. 9:29; 26:8)

CHAPTER 7
THE LIGHT AND THE LAMPS

"There was a man sent from God, whose name was John. The same came for a witness, to bear witness of the Light, that all men through him might believe. He was not that Light, but was sent to bear witness of that Light. That was the true Light, which lighteth every man that cometh into the world". (John 1:6-9)

John, the writer of the "Gospel according to John", was a beloved disciple of Lord Jesus Christ. He writes about John the Baptist, who was a forerunner of Lord Jesus, heralding the coming of Jesus into this world. Earlier, John described Lord Jesus as the "Word", who was with God, and the very God Himself. He was in the world He was the light; but the world comprehended him not. John the Baptist bore witness of that great light, in order that all men through him might believe that Jesus Christ is the Son of God. He bore witness of the Lord and he was not that Light of whom he spoke of. The true light was Lord Jesus Christ, who lightens everyone who takes birth in this world, irrespective of whether one is Jew or Gentile.

There was in Jerusalem a man, whose name was Simeon. He was just and devout waiting for the consolation of Israel. Holy Spirit, who was upon him, revealed to him that he, will not die before he saw Lord Jesus Christ. He went into the temple by the guidance of the Holy Spirit and took into his arms the child Jesus from the arms of Mary and Joseph and blessed the child. He prayed to God and said that he saw the LORD's salvation that the LORD prepared for all mankind. He said that the child was the Light to lighten the Gentiles and the Lord was the glory of the LORD's people Israel. He then sought permission from God to leave this world in peace.

"A light to lighten the Gentiles, and the glory of thy people Israel". (Luke 2:32)

It is sad that even though Lord Jesus came into this world to lighten everyone with the truth, yet men loved darkness rather than light, because they delighted in the deeds of evil more than the deeds of the righteous God. (cf. John 3:19)

Therefore, when Jesus said "you are the light of the world" the phrase meant that men lightened by Him were the reflection of His light. No one in the world can boast that he/she is the true light capable of lightening anyone. Lord Jesus is the only true light and He was divine, who lived among in the likeness of man. (cf. Matt. 5:14)

Lord Jesus Christ is the true light not only now, but He will be the true light in heaven, as well there will be no sun or moon in heaven, the light that would be in heaven is the light from the Lord Jesus Christ.   He is the light of the world, and he is the only one who renders the truth of the knowledge of salvation. He is the only one who offered Himself as sacrifice on behalf of men in order that man may believe in Him and receive salvation.

The Lord said to His disciples that they are, by virtue of the light they have received from the Lord, are the light of the world. They were required to shine in the world as the reflection of the true light. They were required to exhibit to the world the radiance of the glory of the Lord. As they bear the light, the reflection of the true light, which cannot be hid, they were the witnesses of the Lord. They were like a city on a summit that cannot be hid. He who follows the Lord will not walk in darkness. In the Lord is life; and the life was the light of men. As disciples followed Jesus Christ and stood for the truth we the believers in the Lord are required to reflect the light of the Lord (cf. John 1:4, 8; 3:19; 8:12; 9:5, 12:35-36).

The Lord said that no one lights a candle and keeps it under a bushel; rather he places it on a candlestick in order that the light may shine to everyone around. It projects its inherent attribute of making objects visible. The light affords illumination. The Lord gave this example to his disciples and said to them that they should illuminate the people in the world in order that they find the knowledge of the truth by their diligent search for it (cf. Matt.5:15)

There are clear instructions here from the Lord to His followers that they should be wise enough to place themselves as instruments in the hands of God, who may use them in the ways He desires. He is the light and we are the lamps lit by His light. When man submits to the will of God, He uses them to reflect the radiance of His glory before men. The life of believers should be directed in such a manner that the darkness is thwarted away. Indeed, even when a speck of light enters a dark room it lights the whole room bright. Men around believers should be able to see their good works and glorify the Father in heaven.

Never should believers behave as Pharisees did during the period of Lord Jesus, when He was on this earth. Pharisees were, as Jesus called them, were hypocrites, showing off their position in the society to gain importance and glory for themselves. They wore phylacteries, long coats and stood in the corners of the cities to be seen by men. They desired to be called as religious.

The Lord said everyone should love God with all his/her heart, with all his/her soul, and with entire strength; and likewise love one's neighbor as one himself/herself. His followers are required to show longsuffering, goodness, faith, meekness, temperance and have joy and peace.

Apostle Paul reiterated these attributes and said we have to show these fruits of the Spirit before men in order that the Father in heaven may be glorified through the only savior, Lord Jesus Christ. (Matt. 5:16; Gal. 5:22-26)

"Let your light so shine before men, that they may see your good works, and glorify your Father which is in heaven" (Matthew 5:16)

CHAPTER 8
THE UNIQUE GOSPEL

The Gospel according to John has excellent details for preaching to the world, the Gospel of Lord Jesus Christ. While the three synoptic Gospels, namely, Matthew, Mark, Luke pick up the details, as they finding it interesting them, of Lord Jesus Christ at certain points of His life, John goes beyond the description of synoptic Gospels unto the period even beyond the world began. (Synopsis means "a brief or condensed statement giving a general view of some subject" and synoptic Gospels are those which take a common view. This is especially in regard to the life of Jesus and His ministry recorded in the Gospels according to Matthew, Mark, and Luke).

John may have had in front of him the details of synoptic Gospels; yet he omitted many of them in his Gospel, and accommodated many more interesting life-events of Lord Jesus Christ. That is the reason why John's Gospel is distributed to the public, in a small booklet form, in preference to the Gospels according to Matthew, Mark and Luke.

Synoptic Gospels are as much relevant to proclaim the Gospel of Jesus Christ, and yet inasmuch as John takes us back to the events even before the creation of the world, the Gospel of John is preferred more for proclaiming the Gospel Message. John's Gospel convicts the reader or listener greatly and increases his/her faith in Lord Jesus Christ.

Matthew chose to start his gospel with the lineage of Jesus, while Mark starts his Gospel with the life of John the Baptist, who was forerunner of Jesus. John the Baptist says Jesus, who comes after him, was preferred before him, because Jesus was and is the true light of the world. John the Baptist says he was not worthy to unloose the latchet of Lord Jesus Christ. He starts with the Baptism of Jesus. Luke starts his Gospel with the details of the birth of John the Baptist, and thereafter of the Lord Jesus and the beginning of Jesus's ministry on this earth.

Unlike the three Gospel writers, John starts the Gospel with a grand statement as follows:

"In the beginning was the Word, and the Word was with God, and the Word was God" (John 1:1)

Thus, he goes beyond creation narrative written in Genesis 1, which reads...

"In the beginning God created the heaven and the earth". (Genesis 1:1)

It is evident from the statement of John that Lord Jesus existed even before the creation, and He is the creator. The Lord has neither the beginning nor the end; He is always eternal and beyond time. He is everlasting and He is the Son of God and very God Himself. John goes further to state that the Word became flesh and He dwelt among men. He was the "Lamb of God", and He was the one who was to come to save mankind from their sin.

The beginning of the Gospel according to John presents the deity of Lord Jesus Christ, and so does the ending of his book. Thomas, one of the disciples of Jesus, confessed that Jesus was his Lord and his God.

John had ample material to write, and if he did, "the world itself could not contain the books that should be written". Truly, it is so, inasmuch as we see the volumes of explanations of Lord Jesus Christ written by writers, from the limited details mentioned by John, and other Gospel writers, are so vast that the explanations, and expositions keep increasing rather than diminishing. The Word of God is ever fresh and never could it be archived. None of the books in the world can claim this kind achievement. As John puts it..."these are written, that ye might believe that Jesus is the Christ, the Son of God; and that believing ye might have life through his name"

"And after eight days again his disciples were within, and Thomas with them: then came Jesus, the doors being shut, and stood in the midst, and said, Peace be unto you. Then saith he to Thomas, Reach hither thy finger, and behold my hands; and reach hither thy hand, and thrust it into my side: and be not faithless, but believing. And Thomas answered and said unto him, My Lord and my God. Jesus saith unto him, Thomas, because thou hast seen me, thou hast believed: blessed are they that have not seen, and yet have believed. And many other signs truly did Jesus in the presence of his disciples, which are not written in this book: But these are written, that ye might believe that Jesus is the Christ, the Son of God; and that believing ye might have life through his name" (John 20:26-31)

"And there are also many other things which Jesus did, the which, if they should be written every one, I suppose that even the world itself could not contain the books that should be written. Amen" (John 21:25)

Some of the life events mentioned in synoptic Gospels is omitted by John. Those events are...

- The temptation of Jesus
- The transfiguration of Jesus
- Institution of Lord' Supper
- Casting out demons from the afflicted
- The Sermon on the Mount
- Lord's prayer (the sample)

Inclusion by John, of some material that was not found in synoptic Gospels is...

- Lord Jesus ministry in Galilee
- Resurrection of Lazarus
- Lord's farewell speech found in John chapters 13-17
- One to one Ministry with Samaritan woman
- Usage of symbolism such as in John 2:25; 7:37-38; 12:32
- Emphasis more on eternal life rather than "Kingdom of God" or "Kingdom of heaven"

John uses the word "Life" 36 times, whereas Matthew, Mark and Luke use only 7 times, 4 times, and 5 times respectively, while John uses the "kingdom" only 5 times whereas Matthew, Mark and Luke use 55 times, 20 times and 46 times respectively.

[References: John 1:1-18; Genesis 1:1; John Chapters 2-4; John 2:17,22,25,; John Chapters 3,4 and 6; John 7:37-38; John 8:24,28,58; John chapters 11; John 12:16,32; John 1:4; 3:19; 8:12;11:9; 12:35,46; 8:44; 5:24; 11:25; 8:23,33,36; John Chapters 13-17; John 20:9; John 20:25; 21:25; 21:23-24]

CHAPTER 9
THE LAST ADAM PART I

"And so it is written, The first man Adam was made a living soul; the last Adam was made a quickening spirit" (1 Corinthians 15:45)

INTODUCTION

Gospel writer Luke says in Luke 3:38 that Adam was the son of God. Notice lower case "s" was used in the word "son". Therefore, there should be no confusion that he was a man, and yet called as "son of God". Luke was tracing lineage of Lord Jesus Christ, the Son of God, born of the Virgin Mary, conceived in her by the Holy Spirit.

The power of the Highest overshadowed Mary, and, therefore, Jesus was called the "Son of God". Notice the upper case "S" was used in the case of Lord Jesus Christ.

While Adam was the "son of God" by virtue of being created as the first man on this earth, Lord Jesus was the "Son of God" by virtue of His incarnation in the likeness of man. Although He was the very God, the "Wonderful, The mighty God, The everlasting Father, The Prince of Peace", (cf. Isaiah 9:6), yet He was called the "Son of God". One of the Titles of Lord Jesus Christ is "The everlasting Father". Jesus said "I and my Father are one" (John 10:30).

Lord Jesus came unto His own and His own did not receive Him; but to all those who received Him, the Lord gave power to become 'sons of God' (cf. John 1:11, 12)

Gospel writer Matthew traced back the lineage of Lord Jesus until Abraham, Luke traced the lineage of the Lord's back until Adam; but John traced His lineage until before the world began (Ref. John 1:1)

It is evident from the scriptures that Lord Jesus Christ was there with the Father in eternity. The Father, the Son, and the Holy Spirit are eternal, and there is neither beginning nor end to them. They are one in three and had different roles to play in the lives of men. They are co- equal, co-existent.

THE FIRST ADAM

If we carefully ponder on the phrase "And God said, Let us make man in our image, after our likeness", it is evident that plural was used in the case of God, and yet God is one. God determined to make man and designed man in His own image, The LORD God formed man of the dust of the ground, and breathed into his nostrils the breath of life; and man became a living soul (cf. Genesis 1:26; 2:7).

After creating man and the woman, who were Adam and Eve, the LORD blessed them said to them to be fruitful, multiply, replenish the earth, subdue it, and have "dominion over the fish of the sea, over the fowl of the air, over the cattle, overall the earth, every creeping thing that creeps upon the earth" (cf. Gen 1:26).

Not only God gave so much authority to man made out of dust, but He gave the man privilege to be called as the 'son of God' ('s' of "son" in lower case). The LORD created man for His glory (cf. Isa. 43:7; 64:8). He formed man, and made the man. The LORD is the potter and we are the work of His hand. The LORD cherished to have fellowship with man. He communed with man freely more than any good friend would do to us.

GOOD AND EVIL

Man is either guided by the Holy Spirit or by the Evil Spirit; there is no midway. God's Sprit will prevent man to commit sin, and will surely help man to get out of temptation and escape from sin; and yet if man is bent upon committing sin, (which is transgression of God's commandment or Law either of verbal or of written), the LORD's Spirit will not force a man to oppose evil Spirit, but will leave man to take his decision.

It is when man yields to the temptation of the Devil that Evil Spirit takes control of man and leads him into destruction. Satan by nature is a deceiver, and when man yields to his temptation, God stays away from rebellious attitude of man and hands over to his vile desires (cf. Romans 1:21-32). It is then that Satan appears to him as if he is helping him; but ultimately he destroys man.

God did not create Satan or Evil. God called His creation good, and everything He created was good. He created angels, beautiful angels, of which the chief of very beautiful, and he was very good in appearance; but this beautiful chief angel devised evil in his heart to become like God and to take control over him. It is then that God cast him away from His presence and this chief beautiful angel became the worst deceiver, an adversary of God and man.

ADAM AND EVE

God gave commandment to Adam, the first man on this earth. Eve was not physically present at the time when God gave commandment to Adam, but she was in Adam, in his spirit, in his flesh, and in his bones. God caused deep sleep to fall on Adam, and while he was asleep, the LORD took a bone out of his bones and made woman out of it. Adam said "This is now bone of my bones, and flesh of my flesh: she shall be called Woman, because she was taken out of Man" (Ref. Genesis 2:23).

 When the LORD gave commandment to Adam that he can eat of every tree of the garden freely, but not of the tree of the knowledge of good and evil, Eve was inside of Adam, and heard of the commandment of God. The LORD said that in the day when Adam eats it he will surely die.

THE SERPENT

Of any beast in the field that the LORD God made, the serpent was more subtle and cunning. The devil inside of the Serpent posed a very tricky question to the woman by saying, "Yea, hath God said, Ye shall not eat of every tree of the garden? The woman answered and said that they may eat of the fruit of the trees of the garden, but not of the tree which is in the midst of the garden. She quoted God saying "Ye shall not eat of it; neither shall ye touch it, lest ye die". (Genesis 3:2-3), Satan immediately seized the opportunity and took undue advantage of her weakness in yielding. The serpent said to her that they will not surely die, because, according to the devil, their eyes will be opened, and they will be like gods, knowing good and evil (cf. Genesis 3:4-5)

Eve saw that the tree was to be desired to make one wise; that tree was good for food; and it was pleasant in appearance to the eyes. She took her own decision. Yielding to Satan's temptation the woman not only ate it, but also gave to her husband, who also ate it.

It was not man who fell into sin first, but the woman, and yet knowing very well that eating that fruit is transgression of God's commandment, he ate it yielding to the words of the woman, whose spirit was controlled by the Devil.

Thus Adam and Eve transgressed the commandment of God. They yielded to the temptation of Satan. Noticeable fact is that God did not prevent them to eat but He gave a very stern warning that they should not forbidden fruit.

The inference, without any reluctance is that God did not make man as puppet, but gave the privilege for man to choose good or evil according to his willpower. Apostle Paul wrote in 1 Corinthians 10:13 that there is no temptation which is not common to man, and God will not suffer man to be tempted beyond his capability to resist it. Instead the LORD provides a way out to escape from temptation.

In the Case of Job it was God, who challenged Satan to test him and not touch his soul. Therefore, Satan could not kill Job, but tempted him grievously and yet Job did not curse God. In the case of Adam and Eve, God as a Sovereign one had the authority to prove man.

The LORD did not tell Satan to tempt Adam and Eve. It was Satan cunningly tempted Adam and Eve. The man and the woman yielded to his temptation. Therefore, all the three were guilty before God, according to God's standards. And God punished them severely as we read in Genesis 3:9-24

CHAPTER 10
THE LAST ADAM - PART II

NOT A SMALL TRASGRESSION!

Adam's transgression was not a small one to be ignored of by the LORD. The sovereign LORD, who made a man from the dust, gave a command to him for him to obey and not to commit sin against God present excuses to Him. The Serpent, Eve and Adam paid heavily for their transgression, and it is not yet over. The LORD God said to the serpent that it will crawl upon its belly its entire life, and will eat dust all its days. The LORD God said to the woman that she will travail in child birth, and to the man The LORD God said that he shall toil in his life to earn bread.

It was not a command from any human being that if it is violated only body could be killed but not soul, but it was a command from the Almighty God. However, God in His compassion, provided a way for salvation.

The LORD said, in the day man commits transgression against the LORD he will die. The death here means eternal separation of fellowship with God, and physical death. There is no escape from being cast into lake of fire, prepared for Satan and his followers, unless they are saved by the grace of God. What a pathetic situation is that unsaved will receives place in the "lake of fire" along with Satan and his followers.

Man needs to fear God who can kill not only the physical body of man but also cause his soul to be cast into the 'lake of fire', where gnashing of teeth does not cease nor does the fire quench. When Lord Jesus Christ returns the dead in Christ shall rise first, and thereafter those believers in Christ who are alive will be caught to be with the Lord forever and ever in their glorious bodies transformed in a time span of twinkling of an eye.

As for the unbelievers they will also rise at the end of age in their physical bodies, which may or may not be of dust that was used when God created Adam and Eve. Scriptures, as we read in the case of Lazarus and rich man give us indication that rich man had physical body and begged for a droplet of water from Lazarus, who was in the bosom of Abraham. The description given by Jesus does not say that it was a parable but he spoke of reality by mentioning their names.

Adam's transgression was covered by God when He wrapped their bodies with the skin of slain animal showing the future atonement of Lord Jesus Christ under whose righteousness the believers will be made righteous.

As for man desirous of being saved it is as simple as confessing Jesus Christ as Lord and by believing that God raised Him from the dead on the third day. (cf. Romans 10:9-10)

CHAPTER 11
THE BREAD OF LIFE

"I am that bread of life" (John 6:48)

Lord Jesus Christ said He is the bread of Life. What does the 'bread of life' actually mean? What we usually understand is that the bread is food item that supports life. Reading through the context (john 6:47-51) where this verse appears it is evident that Lord Jesus Christ was making a firm affirmation that he who believes on Him has everlasting life.

The Lord was not saying that our physical bodies will remain as they are. He was also not saying that we will not have physical death. Everyman has to die once, but the death in the case of believers, it is different. Their souls will immediately be with the Lord and they do not die to the literal meaning, which is cessation of life once for all.

Jesus was crucified on the cross amidst two thieves on one either side. This was done to insult Him. When He was on the cross, the thief on one side mocked at Jesus but the second thief understood the Jesus is the Lord and Savior. He acknowledged this fact and said they (the two thieves) deserved death, but the righteous Lord did not deserve death; and he turned to the Lord and prayed that the Lord may remember him when He comes in His kingdom. The Lord immediately promised to the second thief that he would be with the Lord on the same day in Paradise.

From the words of Lord Jesus Christ it is evident that death of believer in Christ is not cessation of life, but as it is as it may be called a "Sleep". Lord Jesus used this term in John 11:11. However, later referring to the physical death of Lazarus, the Lord said in John 11:14 that Lazarus was dead.

These things said he: and after that he saith unto them, Our friend Lazarus sleepeth; but I go, that I may awake him out of sleep. (John 11:11)

Then said Jesus unto them plainly, Lazarus is dead. (John 11:14)

Lord Jesus Christ raised Lazarus from his physical death, which was his sleep.

When Jesus said that He was the bread of the life, He meant that He was the source for spiritual life in a believer. Earlier in John 6:35 Jesus said to them that He is 'the bread of life' and whoever comes to Him shall never hunger nor thirst.

While speaking to Samaritan woman in John 4:14 the Lord said, whoever drinks water from the well would thirst, but the water that He gives will be a well of water springing up into everlasting life. The Lord Jesus says that He is the support of spiritual life. He who believes in Him shall have His Spirit in abundance, and His life will be fruitful.

To be born-again, as Jesus said, one has to be born of water and spirit. Physical birth once in this world is not enough to enter into the Kingdom of God, but it is imperative that everyone has to be born-again; that is to say that everyone has to be born of the spirit. Unless a man is born again he cannot see the kingdom of God.

It is not enough for a believer to remain as a babe in Christ, after he is born-again, but he has to grow spiritually. Hebrews 5:13-14 says that strong meat belongs to one who is full of age but everyone, who uses milk, is unskillful in the word of righteousness because he is babe.

When Jesus was tempted in the wilderness, as recorded in Matthew 4:4, He said that man shall not live by bread alone, but every word that comes out of the mouth of God.

Physical needs of Elijah the prophet were met with, when God sent raven with food for him and provided water from the brook of Cherith, which was before Jordan. Ravens brought meat in the morning and bread and meat in the evening, and he drank from the brook when there was no rain the land. (Cf. 1 Kings 17:2-7)

Five thousand men were fed by five loaves and two fishes miraculously by Lord Jesus during His ministry in Galilee. The Lord had gone over the sea of Galilee, which was the sea of Tiberias, and great multitude followed him (John 6:1-14).

In order to see that they may not forcibly take Jesus and make Him king over them, he left them He went to the mountain again (Jews knew that a prophet would come and be their king). His disciples entered into a ship and went over the sea toward Capernaum. It was dark, and the sea arose of a great storm. When they had rowed about thirty furlongs, Jesus came to them by walking on the water. The disciples and the others were afraid looking at Him walk on calm waters. They were in the midst of great wind that blew while they were sailing. Lord Jesus comforted them and said to them that it was He who was coming to them, and therefore, they need not be afraid. They all received the Lord into the ship, and immediately the ship landed safely at the place where they wished to be (cf. 6:17-21).

JEWS CONFRONT JESUS

Next day people saw Jesus and inquired of him "Rabbi, when camest thou hither?" They had gone there by boats from Tiberias, where they ate miraculous food that the Lord provided them. They showed their concern as if they were indeed intently seeking Him; but Jesus said to them that they were not there to see Him or to seek His welfare, but they inquired of Him because they had food miraculously from Him on the other side of the sea. (Ref. John 6:25, 26).

Jesus knew their inward thoughts and, therefore, said to them that they should not labor for worldly food that perishes, but to labor for the meat that endures unto everlasting life, which Lord Jesus, who is the Son of God, alone shall give unto them. He said to them that the Father has appointed His Son alone for this purpose, and that He is the Son of God, who came down from heaven, in the likeness of man (cf. John 6:27)

Jews did not understand what Jesus was speaking about. They inquired as to how they should do the works of God. The Lord answered them and said that they should believe in Him, and that belief will be enough evidence that they are doing the work of God. Jews, then cited as to how their fathers received "Manna" (food from heaven), by the power of God, in the wilderness, at the behest of Moses. They questioned Him as to what sign He would show that they believe Him as the Son of God, the incarnate God.

Lord Jesus quoted Deuteronomy 8:3 and said to them that God provided them food for their physical needs, and humbled them; however, all of them after eating "Manna", died physical death as everyone dies; however, He continued saying that man does not live by bread alone, but by the every word that comes out of the mouth of the LORD.

Of His provision of food that He would give to the world, Lord Jesus said that He is "the bread of life" and He gives everlasting life. They were again confused and prayed to give that bread to them that they live forever on this earth. However, Lord Jesus Christ was saying to them they should believe in Him and receive Him as the Lord and Savior that they may have everlasting life.

As Paul later explains we will be raised with glorified bodies in the twinkling of an eye, when the Lord comes again. He will conform us to His image and we will be with Him forever and ever. He reiterated that He came down from heaven to do the will of the Father, who sent Him into this world in the likeness of man, and that whoever comes to Him will in wise be cast out, but raise him from the dead at the last day.

Jews murmured because Lord Jesus said to them that He is 'the bread of life' that came down from heaven. They wondered if He was not the son of Joseph and Mary, whom they knew. Lord Jesus answered and said to them that they should not murmur among themselves, but to believe in Him as their Savior, who gives them the everlasting life. Jews again murmured as to how the Lord could give them his flesh to eat. The Lord said to them that whosoever eats His flesh and drinks of His blood will live in Him and He in him and he will live forever (cf. John 6:28-59)

"Verily, verily, I say unto you, He that believeth on me hath everlasting life. I am that bread of life" (John 6:47-48)

CHAPTER 12
SUN AND MOON ARE NOT GODS

"And the LORD said unto Moses, Stretch out thine hand toward heaven, that there may be darkness over the land of Egypt, even darkness which may be felt. And Moses stretched forth his hand toward heaven; and there was a thick darkness in all the land of Egypt three days: They saw not one another, neither rose any from his place for three days: but all the children of Israel had light in their dwellings" (Exodus 10:21-23)

For light to shine in the dwelling places of the children of Israel in Egypt, when they were under slavery neither Sun or Moon were required. In the same region where Egyptians lived and the children of Israel lived, there was utter darkness for Egyptians, and there was light for the children of Israel. It happened when Moses by the word of God and by the LORD's Almighty power brought darkness over Pharaoh and his people in Egypt. It was ninth plague that God sent over Pharaoh and his people in the land of Egypt.

There was another important incident after the deliverance of the children of Israel from the bondage of slavery in Egypt, able leaders of Egyptians led by Pharaoh chased the children of Israel from behind to catch hold of them and take them back to Egypt to work for him and Egyptians, as slaves.

Pharaoh and war-experts in their chariots, perhaps, forgot their sufferings when God had put them to terrible sufferings by bringing on them the ten plagues. Of the Ten plagues, the last plague was indeed terrible one for them. The first born of

Egyptians including that of Pharaoh were killed by the LORD because Pharaoh went back on his word nine times earlier that he would release the children of Israel from the bondage of slavery, but did not keep up his word.

Pharaoh hardened his heart and therefore, God hardened his heart that the LORD may show His almighty power over Egyptians. Pharaoh was humiliated when the LORD killed his firstborn. He released the children of Israel and while they were on their way to the Promised Land, Pharaoh shamelessly followed them, in vain, to take them back to Egypt.

It was at that time that the Angel of God, who went before the camp of Israel moved to be behind them, and the pillar of the cloud went from before their face stood behind them. It was between the camp of Egyptians and the camp of Israel. For Egyptians the cloud was darkness to them, but it gave light by night to the children of Israel.

Thus, neither Egyptians could come near the children of Israel nor the children of Israel could go near them. The LORD controlled whole situation. The sun and moon were nowhere near the Egyptians to help The LORD was the light for the children of Israel and made the Egyptians to grope in darkness.

The children of Israel with all their cattle walked on the dry ground between the Red Sea which was, in the meanwhile, parted into two by Moses by the power of the Almighty God. After the children of Israel safely passed onto the other shore of the Red Sea, the Egyptians attempted to cross the Red Sea on the dry land, but alas! Moses lifted his staff once again invoking God's power, and the LORD brought waters together. Pharaoh, and his men in the chariots, were drowned in the Red Sea and got killed; never again to follow the children of Israel.

God is all-powerful. When He said "Let there be light", "there was light" and God saw that the light was good and He divided the light from the darkness, and thus God created time, as well. Sun and moon were placed by God in the firmament to help man to distinguish days, months and seasons. Sun and Moon were not the source of light, but they were the source to differentiate times and seasons. The Time is also, therefore, a creation of God. Neither Sun nor Moon or Time is gods; but they were creation of God. (cf. Genesis 1:3-5; 1:14).

God said...

"Thou shalt have no other gods before me. Thou shalt not make unto thee any graven image, or any likeness of any thing that is in heaven above, or that is in the earth beneath, or that is in the water under the earth" (Exodus 20:3-4)

In the New Testament God's judgment of sin was seen at the cross of Calvary where Lord Jesus Christ was crucified in our stead in order that we may have redemption from sin. From sixth hour to ninth hour, which according to our time in the present days, is from 12:00 PM to 3:00 PM there was utter darkness. The sun was darkened. It pleased the Father to bruise the Son, Lord Jesus Christ, who knew no sin but was made sin for us, in order that we might be made righteousness of God in Him (cf. Luke 23:44-46, 2 Corinthians 5:21)

Salvation is free of cost. Bible says...

"That if thou shalt confess with thy mouth the Lord Jesus, and shalt believe in thine heart that God hath raised him from the dead, thou shalt be saved. For with the heart man believeth unto righteousness; and with the mouth confession is made unto salvation" (Romans 10:9-10)

CHAPTER 13
PARABLE OF THE SOWER

And when he sowed, some seeds fell by the way side, and the fowls came and devoured them up: Some fell upon stony places, where they had not much earth: and forthwith they sprung up, because they had no deepness of earth: And when the sun was up, they were scorched; and because they had no root, they withered away. And some fell among thorns; and the thorns sprung up, and choked them: But other fell into good ground, and brought forth fruit, some an hundredfold, some sixtyfold, some thirtyfold. (Matthew 13:4-8)

The essence of the parable of the sower, as described in three synoptic Gospels by three different writers was to show how Satan does not allow weak in heart and mind to obey the word of God and tempts not to yield to the Lord.

It is the same parable from Lord Jesus Christ that the three Gospel writers presented in similar way except that Matthew used a phrase at one place as the "kingdom of heaven" while Mark and Luke called it as "kingdom of God".

This parable is not presenting to us a theme as to what the local church and the universal church are, as a preacher described them as, based on two different phrases that is the "kingdom of heaven" and the "kingdom of God" respectively. He said "kingdom of heaven" is the local church and "kingdom of God" is the "Universal Church".

The Scriptures make it clear that Christ is the head of the Church (Ekklesia) and we are all baptized into one body. There is no difference in His body, whether we are Jews, or Gentiles, are bond or free, men or women. Local church is an entity in a local area, but it is not separate from the body of Christ. Church is not a building with four or more walls but it is the body of Christ. It is as the Greek Strong's number 1577 "ekklesia" defines it and the definition is:

"a calling out, i.e. (concretely) a popular meeting, especially a religious congregation (Jewish synagogue, or Christian community of members on earth or saints in heaven or both):-- assembly, church"

Lord Jesus Christ said He will build Church upon Himself and the gates of hell will not prevail against it. If Christ has said those words, then there is no other interpretation that the Church will diminish or reduce in growth, no matter how effectively or how ineffectively a preacher presents the Word of God.

"And I say also unto thee, That thou art Peter, and upon this rock I will build my church; and the gates of hell shall not prevail against it". (Matthew 16:18)

For as the body is one, and hath many members, and all the members of that one body, being many, are one body: so also is Christ. For by one Spirit are we all baptized into one body, whether we be Jews or Gentiles, whether we be bond or free; and have been all made to drink into one Spirit. For the body is not one member, but many. (1 Corinthians 12:12-14)

There is neither Jew nor Greek, there is neither bond nor free, there is neither male nor female: for ye are all one in Christ Jesus. (Galatians 3:28)

The Gospel writers wrote the words of Lord Jesus Christ, who said the 'seed' in this parable represents the Word of God, and the sower is God's servant who proclaims the word of God. There are four categories of people about whom the Lord addresses here in this parable.

The places where the seed fell were described by the Lord as

1. "by the wayside",
2. "upon stony places",
3. "among the thorns" and
4. "into the good ground".

These four places represent four categories of people.

While the Word of God is proclaimed to the world in different places to the men with different yielding attitudes, the prince of this world, that is the Satan, takes undue advantage of the weakness of the hearers, who are reluctant to yield to the word of God, and takes away from them the word of God.

The sower, who is God's servant, who is used by the Lord, as the instrument in His hands, proclaims the Word of God everywhere he goes. He proclaims the Word of God indiscriminately to all categories of people, without any prejudice.

In this parable the Lord says a sower went forth to sow, and as he sowed some seed fell by the way side, and some fell upon stony places, and some fell among thorns.

1. The seed that is the Word of God that fell by the wayside was picked up by the fowls; they devoured it up.

2. The seed that is the Word of God that fell on the stony places could not spring up because there was no depth of earth for the seed to grow its roots and stem. When the sun came up the seed was scorched and withered away.
3. The seed that is the Word of God among the thorns did not spring up because the thorns choked them.
4. The seed that is the Word of God that fell on the good ground brought forth much fruit, some hundredfold, some sixtyfold and some thirtyfold.

Lord Jesus warns that whoever has diligence could open their ears to hear the word of God and hear. Faith comes by hearing and hearing by the word of God.

The seed that fell "by the wayside" shows that those who have heard the Word of God do not take the Word seriously and eventually they allow Satan to takeaway what was sown in their hearts.

The stony places are the hard-heartened hearts of men who receive the Word of God happily with much joy but as there is no root in them, or just as the rock prevents root to grow in it, the man with stony heart will not endure in the Word of God, but when he faces tribulations or persecutions in his life he gives up his holy life in God and leaves the righteous life.

Those who receive the Word of God among the thorns, which represent the care of this world, the deceitfulness of riches, lose their stand in the Lord, because the thorns choke the good seed sown in their hearts and eventually he/she becomes unfruitful.

Gospel writer described it as

"But other fell into good ground, and brought forth fruit, some an hundredfold, some sixtyfold, some thirtyfold". (Matthew 13:8)

Gospel writer Mark described it as:

"And other fell on good ground, and did yield fruit that sprang up and increased; and brought forth, some thirty, and some sixty, and some an hundred". (Mark 4:8)

Gospel writer Luke described it as:

"And other fell on good ground, and sprang up, and bare fruit an hundredfold. And when he had said these things, he cried, He that hath ears to hear, let him hea". (Luke 8:8)

Careful observation shows that Matthew presented the increase in reverse order, i.e. as "brought forth fruit, some an hundredfold, some sixtyfold, some thirtyfold", while Mark presented it as "and brought forth, some thirty, and some sixty, and some an hundred" and Luke presented it as "bare fruit an hundredfold" without writing anything as "sixtyfold" or thirtyfold"

Should presentation cause the fact to be represented as diminishing the fruit that the workers or hearers bring forth? No, not at all! Three different authors presented the growth in three different ways. Overall, it showed increase not decrease. It all shows that some were not as fruitful as others and it does not show downward trend.

"So then faith cometh by hearing, and hearing by the word of God". (Romans 10:17)

CHAPTER 14
LIVING SACRIFICE

I beseech you therefore, brethren, by the mercies of God, that ye present your bodies a living sacrifice, holy, acceptable unto God, which is your reasonable service. And be not conformed to this world: but be ye transformed by the renewing of your mind, that ye may prove what is that good, and acceptable, and perfect, will of God. (Romans 12:1-2)

We worship the Lord in Spirit and in Truth by taking part in the Lord's Supper we are reminded how to offer our bodies as living sacrifice, holy and acceptable unto God. This a reasonable service. We are exhorted not to be conformed to this world, but be transformed to the renewing of our minds. We do that in order that we may prove what is that good and what is that acceptable and perfect and the will of God.

As usual Paul makes an appeal saying "I beseech you". He says God is calling us to make choice as to how to live for Him. God has shown us His mercy in giving us salvation free of cost by paying the price for it on the cross. He has paid the debts we owe under the Law and freed us from the demands of the Law.

MERCIES OF GOD

- He has become Propitiation for us and redeemed us, sanctified us and justified us.
- He Set us under Grace redeeming us from the demands of the Law

- He has granted us the gift of the indwelling of the Holy Spirit
- He helps us in afflictions
- He granted us the privilege of not being separated from Him
- He promised us to be conformed to His image.

Therefore, the Lord demands from us to present our bodies living sacrifices to Him. We have body, soul and Spirit. In this context we are asked to bring all the three elements of our beings, the Body, the Soul, and the Spirit before Him as sacrifice.

If we have no self-control over body, it becomes our master. Sacrifice is living. In the Old Testament where we see the animals, which were brought to the altar were living and not dead. In the New Testament we see all these animal sacrifices are set aside by Lord Jesus Christ who became propitiation for us once and for all. He became the mediator of the better covenant. He paid the price on our behalf.

The Lord paid the price for our redemption but we are exempt from bringing our body, soul and spirit as holy acceptable unto God. This is no concession given to us here. It should be similar to Leviticus 1:9, 10 and Deuteronomy 15:21. This is our reasonable service.

CHAPTER 15
JESUS CAME FOR US

"These words spake Jesus, and lifted up his eyes to heaven, and said, Father, the hour is come; glorify thy Son, that thy Son also may glorify thee: As thou hast given him power over all flesh, that he should give eternal life to as many as thou hast given him. And this is life eternal, that they might know thee the only true God, and Jesus Christ, whom thou hast sent" (John 17:1-3)

Lord Jesus submitted Himself to the Father in obedience, as He did always throughout His ministry, and prayed to Him to glorify Him. In His entire ministry Jesus glorified the Father. Although He said in John 14:30 that He and the Father are one, yet Lord Jesus was obedient to the Father in all respects, and did what He did after praying to the Father.

Apostle Paul says in Philippians 2:8 that Jesus humbled Himself and became obedient unto death, even of the cross.

Jesus says His hour has come that He should die for the sins of mankind in order that they may, by confessing Him as the Lord, may receive everlasting life. Paul in Romans 5:6 says that Jesus died, in due time, for the ungodly, who were yet without strength.

Once at Cana feast He said His hour has not come; but now as He prays to the Father He says His hour has come. He came into this world as incarnate God. He came in the form of a servant and in the likeness of a man. He lived among men and suffered during His life time living like an ordinary man.

Although He was from heaven, where He was partaker of the glory of the Father, yet in his fleshly body He bore our sin and our pain.

The Lord suffered on the rugged cross, with nails in his palms and feet, and a crown of thorns on His head. He bore the shame that we should have borne otherwise. There were no thorns when God created the heaven and the earth and all that is in there; but when man sinned the ground turned out to be a curse for man. Beautiful leaves turned as thorns and thistles on plants and trees. The wearing of crown of thorns on His head, signified the suffering and the curse that the Lord bore on our behalf.

It pleased the Father to bruise Him on the cross in order that we may not be bruised for our sins. That was the true love of God. He loved us first; not that we loved Him. The Father gave Him power over all flesh that the Lord may give eternal life to as many as the Father has given Him. Lord Jesus would have accomplished the purpose He came into this world by the time He finished His dying on the cross, which shortly after His prayer He did. His prayer to the Father now was His supplication seeking blessings upon all those who were given to Him by the Father.

The Lord says the life that he gives to believers was eternal and His prayer was that they, the disciples, who were given to Him, may know the Father, the only true God, and Jesus Christ, whom the Father had sent. When Jesus was on the cross dying for the sins of mankind He said "It is finished" signifying that the Lord had fully accomplished the Father's work.

Jesus asserts before the Father that He relinquished His glory that He had before the foundation of the world was created.

Speaking of His disciples that they were chosen and given to Him by the Father and they have known the truth of the knowledge of God and did keep His word. They have not only known that He is the true God, but also known that whatever Lord Jesus had, was all given to Him by the Father.

After His death, burial and resurrection the Lord said to His disciples "... All power is given unto me in heaven and in earth. Go ye therefore, and teach all nations, baptizing them in the name of the Father, and of the Son, and of the Holy Ghost: Teaching them to observe all things whatsoever I have commanded you: and, lo, I am with you alway, even unto the end of the world. Amen" (Matthew 28:18-20)

The Lord was addressing them in John 16:28-33 that He came forth from the Father and will return to Him. The disciples were confused at the saying of Jesus that He came from the Father and he will return to Him. He said that earlier as well. Knowing that His disciples were confused of this saying He made it clear to them that they would have troubles in this world.

The troubles that this world would give to them would be similar to the labor pains of woman until the child is born, but immediately after the child is born her joy leaps endless bounds as she forgets her pain, and her sorrow, which turn into joy. Jesus confides in them that when troubles come into their lives they should not be discouraged but encounter them with joy because their joy in their eternal life with the Lord will inexpressibly be beautiful and wonderful. He says no one could ever take away that joy when they are with Him in eternity conformed to His image (cf. John 16:16-33; Romans 8:29).

While I continued His prayer to the Father, the Lord says He does not pray for the world, and also that He would not pray that disciples be removed from the world for fear of the troubles; but He does pray for them that they may be sanctified through His truth and the word of His truth that they may face any persecution for the Lord. He also prays for all those who would come to Him and believe on Him through their preaching of the Gospel of Jesus Christ.

In that the Lord seeks blessings upon all those who believe in Jesus Christ as Savior that they all may be one as the Father is in the Son, and the Son is in the Father that all believers may be one in Father and the Son.

Lord Jesus Christ says He gave the glory not only to His disciples, but to all those who believe in Him in order that they all may be one. The world did not know these facts and therefore, when the true light came into this world the darkness did not understand the reason for His coming into this world. The Father sent Him and He came into this world.

The Father loved the Son even before the foundation of the world, and not only His disciples but everyone who believes in Him will see the glory that He had even before the foundation of the world. He declared to them the name of the Father and He loved them and seeks from the Father the same kind of love toward them as well.

As believers in the Lord we are assured of glorified bodies transformed from our earthly bodies into heavenly bodies within that span of a twinkling of an eye. He gives a body to each believer that is pleasing unto the Lord, to every seed his own body at our resurrection. The LORD God breathed into the nostrils of the first man and made him a living soul, and he was Adam, who was not spiritual but earthy and natural; but the Lord, who was known as the last Adam, was a quickening spirit and came down from heaven. He gives us glorified bodies to live with Him forever and ever.

We bear the image of the heavenly and inherit the kingdom of God. The corruptible body that we have in this world will turn into incorruptible and will put on immortality. It is then that we say "O death, where is thy sting? O grave, where is thy victory? The sting of death is sin; and the strength of sin is the law" (cf. 1 Corinthians 15:38-58).

CHAPTER 16
A LIVELY HOPE

Peter an Apostle of Lord Jesus Christ writes in his epistle to the scattered Jews comforting them of a lively hope. The question is what kind of hope Peter is writing about?

Unlike others, Christians are given a lively hope that after death, man's life does not cease to exist, but it continues. The dead in Christ will rise, and it is the resurrection of our lives in glorified bodies. Whether one accepts or rejects this truth, it shall come to pass that after our physical death, the life does not cease to exist. The spirit goes back to God, who breathed it into the nostrils of man when He created man. The body which God made out of dust returns to dust, and gets assimilated into the dust; but the soul of every saved one and unsaved one rises from the grave, at an appropriate time appointed by God, either unto life forever, or for condemnation forever respectively. Denying this truth will not alter the truth; but those who deny this truth will remain in darkness.

Peter was not only addressing the scattered Jews among nations when they were greatly persecuted under Nero in AD 67-70, but also to the Gentiles. In 1 Peter 2:9-10 he says we (Jews and Gentiles), were not a people of God, but now have obtained mercy.

"But ye are a chosen generation, a royal priesthood, an holy nation, a peculiar people; that ye should shew forth the praises of him who hath called you out of darkness into his marvellous light: Which in time past were not a people, but are now the people of God: which had not obtained mercy, but now have obtained mercy" (1 Peter 2:9-10)

Our souls do have a resting period, after which they are resurrected. Bible describes of two resurrections. One is that of the saved ones, and the second one is of unsaved ones. What does the saved or unsaved mean?

Saved ones are those who have yielded to the good news of Lord Jesus Christ that He is the only savior and by whom alone there is salvation; and on whom the light of the Lord did shine, whereby they reflect His light. They are those who have accepted Jesus Christ as their Lord, who alone can forgive one's sins when sinner repents of his sin, and confesses Jesus as the Lord, and believes in heart that God raised Him on the third day from the dead. Repentance is turning to God confessing sin. It is the transgression of His Law ('missing the mark') that one has to confess, but the details of every sin. Unsaved ones are those who prefer to remain in darkness by rejecting the Gospel of Lord Jesus Christ and redemption from sin.

Bible says that all have sinned and come short of the glory of God. In the Old Testament period there were sacrifices made on the altar as substitutionary death for salvation, and this continual offering of sacrifices is done away with, when Lord Jesus Christ became perfect sacrifice and our only mediator. He died as our substitute on the cross, on our behalf, in order that by repenting and confessing our sin and accepting Him as the Lord of our lives we may receive salvation.

After death there is a period of rest in the bosom of Abraham for the souls of the saved ones; and they are resurrected in their glorified bodies, when Lord Jesus Christ comes again. The spirit of believers and unbelievers will be with God during the wait period until the Lord comes again

There is a period of wait in heal for unbelievers and the accomplishment of a thousand year reign of Lord Jesus Christ from the throne of David, and after defeating Satan at the 'Armageddon war; the unbelievers are resurrected to face judgment.

They stand at the 'great white throne' on which the Lord is sits, and judges them and casts death and hell along with unsaved ones into the 'lake of fire', where there is no death, but gnashing of teeth and everlasting pain, and groaning.

The lively hope for a Christian, therefore, is that he will be resurrected to life in glorified body to be with the Lord forever and ever, and will be confirmed to His image. The truth is that in eternity we will have no pain, no death, no hurdles to face such as seas; but walk on the street of gold, in that new city of Jerusalem, where there is neither sun nor moon to light the city, but the light of that city is the light coming out of Lord Jesus Christ.

Jesus said...

"For then shall be great tribulation, such as was not since the beginning of the world to this time, no, nor ever shall be" (Matthew 24:21)

"And then shall appear the sign of the Son of man in heaven: and then shall all the tribes of the earth mourn, and they shall see the Son of man coming in the clouds of heaven with power and great glory. And he shall send his angels with a great sound of a trumpet, and they shall gather together his elect from the four winds, from one end of heaven to the other" (Matthew 24:30-31)

Peter says that by the Lord's abundant mercy he has begotten us again unto a lively hope by the resurrection of Jesus Christ from the dead (cf. 1 Peter 1:3)

About the lives of those unsaved ones, John says...

"And the beast was taken, and with him the false prophet that wrought miracles before him, with which he deceived them that had received the mark of the beast, and them that worshipped his image. These both were cast alive into a lake of fire burning with brimstone". (Revelation 19:20)

"And the devil that deceived them was cast into the lake of fire and brimstone, where the beast and the false prophet are, and shall be tormented day and night for ever and ever" (Revelation 20:10)

"And death and hell were cast into the lake of fire. This is the second death" (Revelation 20:14)

"And whosoever was not found written in the book of life was cast into the lake of fire" (Revelation 20:15)

CHAPTER 17
MANSIONS IN FATHER'S HOUSE

"Let not your heart be troubled: ye believe in God, believe also in me. In my Father's house are many mansions: if it were not so, I would have told you. I go to prepare a place for you. And if I go and prepare a place for you, I will come again, and receive you unto myself; that where I am, there ye may be also. And whither I go ye know, and the way ye know. Thomas saith unto him, Lord, we know not whither thou goest; and how can we know the way? Jesus saith unto him, I am the way, the truth, and the life: no man cometh unto the Father, but by me" (John 14:1-6)

Lord Jesus gave commandment to His disciples that they should love one another as He loved them and in doing so, they would be excellent witnesses for the Lord. Thus the world will honor not only them but the Lord, as well. Earlier at the feast of Passover, He said to them that He will leave them and the world, and will go to the Father, from whom He had come into this world as incarnate God. He came to save sinners. He would not leave the world before accomplishing the purpose for which He came nor would He leave them without comforter after He has departed.

Simon Peter, the disciples of Jesus Christ was confused about His saying and asked the Lord as to where He was going. Answering Peter's question the Lord turned to all His disciples and said to them that they would not be able to follow the Lord but they would be with the Lord in due course of time. Peter was astonished and said that He would die for the Lord, but then the Lord showed Him his weakness. Peter was rightly proved that he was fallible when he denied Jesus three times before the cock crew three times the next morning (cf. John 13:34-38).

In this troubling situation, when one of them, whose name was Judas Iscariot, had betrayed the Lord, the disciples were worried about the Lord's saying that He would suffer and will leave them and go to the Father. The Lord consoles them that they should not be troubled but says to them to be assured that He was going to the Father to prepare mansions for them, and that the Father has many mansions in His house.

Here is a thought to ponder on. What did He mean by the saying that He was going to prepare a place for them (and of course for all who believe in Him and that the Father has many mansions in His house? This was indeed perplexing to them, and it could be perplexing now to us, as well. How could be there many mansions in a house?

God is sovereign. He is omniscient and omnipotent. That is to say God is everywhere; whether it is in heaven, or on earth, or on Mars, or Jupitar, God is everywhere. He created everything, and everything is inside of Him.

King Solomon, while dedicating the Temple He built for God, wonders in his prayer as to whether God can be accommodated in the Temple he built for God. He recollects that heaven is God's throne and earth is God's footstool.

"But will God indeed dwell on the earth? behold, the heaven and heaven of heavens cannot contain thee; how much less this house that I have builded?" (1 Kings 8:27)

The Almighty God says…

"Thus saith the LORD, The heaven is my throne, and the earth is my footstool: where is the house that ye build unto me? and where is the place of my rest?" (Isaiah 66:1)

Stephen in his speech before the high priest recounts the saga King Solomon made in building the Temple for the LORD, and says God made everything and no earthly building can hold Him inside of any building that they make for God or confine Him to a place.

"But Solomon built him an house. Howbeit the most High dwelleth not in temples made with hands; as saith the prophet, Heaven is my throne, and earth is my footstool: what house will ye build me? saith the Lord: or what is the place of my rest? Hath not my hand made all these things?" (Acts 7:47-50)

If so, the question remains as to where our souls would go after our death! The physical body is made of dust to house soul and spirit. When our physical bodies cease to exist it becomes one with the dust of this earth. The soul and spirit will leave the physical body. Physical body is made of dust and therefore, it returns to the dust, and when it does, it is incapable of holding soul and spirit of the man. The soul is the living actuating force of a man; it is the inner man, who lives forever and ever. The soul and spirit of man never ceases to exist. They will remain somewhere and that somewhere is within God's realm.

From rich man and Lazarus real lives Lord Jesus has shown to us that believers' bodies will raised with spirit and soul in them to be received by the Lord forever and ever. Paul also writes about the dead bodies of believers and the living being raised from the grave to be with the Lord forever and ever. Both ultimately receive glorified bodies and these glorified bodies with soul and spirit constitute the complete redemption of man from sin, and only these bodies will see Lord Jesus face to face, and are qualified to be with the Lord forever and ever. These glorified, imperishable bodies with soul and spirit in them will be conformed to the image of Lord Jesus Christ and to live forever and ever

The body of unsaved person will also be raised from the graves to be condemned of the evil he/she has done in his/her life. Although the body returns to grave and get assimilated with the dust, yet it rises when it is time for the Lord to judge the souls of unsaved souls at the great white throne. The unsaved thus judged will be cast into the 'lake of fire', where fire never quenches and gnashing of teeth never ceases.

Thus it is seen that even though the physical body ceases to exist for a time it will be raised at an appropriate time appointed by God. The rich man and Lazarus story is not a fable or parable, but it is a reality. The soul of the saved one will be in the Abraham's bosom and the soul of an unsaved will be in a place of torment, where there is no consolation. There is a great gulf between these two categories of people, and yet they can communicate with one another.

Rich man requested Abraham that Lazarus who was in his bosom, may bring a droplet of water and wet his tongue in order to quench his thirst. That indeed shows that their soul does not cease to exist even after their physical bodies ceased to exist. While they remained at great distance they had some form of bodies; but not physical bodies as we do have now (cf. Luke 16:20-31)

CHAPTER 18
MANSIONS IN FATHER'S HOUSE –
Part II

In my Father's house are many mansions: if it were not so, I would have told you. I go to prepare a place for you. And if I go and prepare a place for you, I will come again, and receive you unto myself; that where I am, there ye may be also. (John 14:2-3)

There are varied interpretations about the mansions in the Father's house. Some think that there are physical buildings in heaven, but careful reading shows that mansions referred to in these verses are not physical buildings, but they are dwelling places in the Father's house. As we, who will be raised from the dead with glorified bodies, which can pass the physical walls, and be present instantly in the time span of twinkling of an eye with the Lord Jesus Christ, there is no scope of believing that we are going to live in physical buildings in eternity.

Lord Jesus Christ, after His resurrection entered a house that had closed doors and wished His disciples peace.

"Then the same day at evening, being the first day of the week, when the doors were shut where the disciples were assembled for fear of the Jews, came Jesus and stood in the midst, and saith unto them, Peace be unto you" (John 20:19)

Inasmuch as we will be with Lord Jesus Christ forever having been conformed to His image, we do not need physical locations and physical buildings just the Lord does not any need of them.

The shadow of this kind of different body is seen when angels visited Abraham and Lot. Three men, out of which, one was pre-incarnate Jesus, visited Abraham to give him good tidings that He will have a son, who will inherit blessings and will bring forth multitudes of people in numbers of the size of uncountable stars and dust of the earth. When Abraham saw three men, he bowed down to the pre-incarnate Jesus and worshipped Him (cf. Genesis18:2).

Abraham lifted his eyes and looked and there were three men stood by him, but he bowed to one of those three men and said to Him "… My Lord, if now I have found favour in thy sight, pass not away, I pray thee, from thy servant." (Genesis 18:3). It is obvious from the scriptures that angels do not accept worship. After Abraham had treated them well, the Lord blessed Abraham. When Sarah laughed the Lord said to Abraham…

"And the LORD said unto Abraham, Wherefore did Sarah laugh, saying, Shall I of a surety bear a child, which am old? Is anything too hard for the LORD? At the time appointed I will return unto thee, according to the time of life, and Sarah shall have a son. (Genesis 18:13-14)

Abraham had communed with the LORD and inquired if He was going to destroy Sodom and Gomorrah. The LORD answered and said if ten righteous men were found in those cities He would not destroy those cities, and the Lord went His way. Other two angels in the form of men visited Lot and communed with him.

From these three angels who appeared to Abraham and two to Lot, it is seen that angels can take the form of men.

Be not forgetful to entertain strangers: for thereby some have entertained angels unawares. (Hebrews 13:2)

Nebuchadnezzar, King of Babylon, commanded that Shadrach, Meshach, and Abednego be cast into fiery furnace, which was heated seven times greater than the usual heat. However, he saw fourth man in the burning fire, and none of them were hurt. Fire had no power over them.

Who was the fourth man? Nebuchadnezzar saw the fourth man and acknowledged that He was the Son of God.

"Then Nebuchadnezzar the king was astonied, and rose up in haste, and spake, and said unto his counsellors, Did not we cast three men bound into the midst of the fire? They answered and said unto the king, True, O king. He answered and said, Lo, I see four men loose, walking in the midst of the fire, and they have no hurt; and the form of the fourth is like the Son of God". (Daniel 3:24-25)

Scripture says that we will walk on the "street of gold" in eternity and live in New Jerusalem, where there is no Sun, or Moon, but there is light is from Lord Jesus Christ, who is the true light and the source of light. From these facts it can be inferred that there are no physical buildings in the Father's house, but there are dwelling places. We do not know where these dwelling places are located; however one thing is sure from the Scriptures that there in the New Jerusalem, the Holy city coming down from heaven, where we have our dwelling.

"And I John saw the holy city, new Jerusalem, coming down from God out of heaven, prepared as a bride adorned for her husband". (Revelation 21:2)

New Jerusalem is the bride of Lord Jesus Christ, and John saw the city coming down from God in heaven. That is the privilege we have in Christ Jesus that we are in Him and He in us.

Jesus answered and said unto him, If a man love me, he will keep my words: and my Father will love him, and we will come unto him, and make our abode with him. (John 14:23)

Paul says about the bodies that God created. There are celestial bodies, terrestrial bodies each one differs in its glory from the other. Sun, Moon and Stars are not identical in their glory, and each star differs from the other (cf. 1 Corinthians 15:40-41). We will rise up from the grave or if be caught up alive if we are alive when Lord Jesus Christ comes again. We will be given glorified bodies of the choice of God, and our glorified bodies will be so viable that we can be instantly at a place where we think of being or at the discretion of the Lord. Revelation 1:6 gives us great hope that we will be kings and priests unto God and His Father.

"And hath made us kings and priests unto God and his Father; to him be glory and dominion for ever and ever. Amen. (Revelation 1:6).

Lord Jesus Christ was the incarnate God fully divine and fully human, and He lived among men, and offered Himself upon the cross as sacrifice on behalf of us. It is by accepting Him as the Lord that we receive everlasting life. He is the only mediator between the Father and us (Ref. Hebrews 10:12). He said to Philp, once that whoever has seen Him has seen the Father. We have the Word of God to meditate upon and see Him in His Word (cf. John 1:1). We will see Him face to face once and be with Him forever and ever in eternity. We will be confirmed to His image and be like Him in eternity.

"But this man, after he had offered one sacrifice for sins forever, sat down on the right hand of God" (Hebrews 10:12)

"For now we see through a glass, darkly; but then face to face: now I know in part; but then shall I know even as also I am known" (1 Corinthians 13:12)

CHAPTER 19
SATAN'S POWERS ARE LIMITED

"And fear not them which kill the body, but are not able to kill the soul: but rather fear him which is able to destroy both soul and body in hell" (Matthew 10:28)

Lord Jesus cautions those who fear excessively of Satan's powers and persecutors in this world. The Lord says fear God who has control of our not only physical bodies but of souls as well. Satan cannot touch believers unless God permits to do so.

Satan is the ruler of this evil world and he filled this earth with sin. The devil tempted Lord Jesus in the wilderness enticing Him with worldly wealth and power; but the Lord did not yield to Satan's temptation. Jesus said to Satan to worship God (Matthew 4:1-11).

Satan knew that Jesus was the Son of God and, therefore, his prime aim was first to ask the Lord to worship him and thereafter murder Him. If Satan knew that the death and resurrection of Jesus would bring salvation to mankind he would never have played a role in the death of Jesus.

Satan was working towards the death of Jesus right from the time when Jesus was born in this world. He played into the mind of Herod to kill infant Jesus, but was not successful. Satan took control of Herod's mind and asked the wise men to get him information about Jesus. Satan's plan through Herod was to murder Jesus, but Satan failed there. (Cf. Matthew 2:1-8)

Harboring the evil thoughts of defeating the Lord by asking Him to worship him, the devil tried to have dominion over the Son of God, but that did not happen. Satan made attempts to kill Jesus though Pharisees by encouraging them to kill the Lord by stoning him to death but the Lord escaped from death because His time had not come.

No one could lay hands on the Lord until He voluntarily allowed the aggressors to capture Him when they came with clubs and swords to arrest Him. The Lord said He was in their midst, doing miracles and teaching and preaching the kingdom of God, and yet they did not believe Him, nor were they arrest Him during those days (cf. John 8:59 and John 10:39).

When it was time for Lord Jesus to lay down His life, He laid it down for our sake, and God raised Him to life when it was Lord's time to rise from the grave. Jesus had the authority over His own life, death and resurrection.

"No man taketh it from me, but I lay it down of myself. I have power to lay it down, and I have power to take it again. This commandment have I received of my Father" (John 10:18).

It is Jesus who has the authority over our lives, death

and resurrection. Satan cannot take our lives nor can hold up in the grave by his authority. Satan is given the power to end the life of a person only under the permission from God. The life span of any person is not controlled by Satan, but it is controlled by God.

Satan had no power to take the life of Jesus because He was sinless. Satan made unlawful attempts to end the life of Jesus and lost his own right to rule over the death. Satan took possession of Judas Iscariot, a disciple of Jesus, and made him to betray Jesus, not surely with the purpose of making provision of salvation to mankind, but to remove him from this earth which would pave way for him to continue to deceive man.

The death of Jesus was prophesied in Isaiah 53 and it pleased the Father to bruise Him for our sake. By the death of Jesus on the Cross for our sake, and by his burial, and by His resurrection without His body getting corrupted, the death was defeated and thus Satan is defeated. This paved the way for mankind to seek salvation through grace by faith in Lord Jesus Christ.

The death could not hold Jesus in the grave but Jesus rose from the dead on the third day. In John 10:17 Jesus emphatically stated that He lays down His life that He might take it again and, therefore, the Father loves him.

"Therefore doth my Father love me, because I lay down my life, that I might take it again". (John 10:17)

Lord Jesus Christ thought it not robbery to be equal

with God, but He took the form of a servant and was made likeness of men. He made himself of no reputation and humbled himself and became obedient unto death, even the most wretched death on the Cross.

It is because Jesus, the Son of God, who was manifest in flesh, humbled Himself so much that He was exalted by God. Jesus was given a name that is above every name and every knee shall bow to him. The authority of Jesus is over everything in heaven, everything in earth and everything under earth, and everything in the Seas (Cf. Philippians 2:6-10).

CHAPTER 20
THE HOLY SPIRIT IN US

"And when he had said this, he breathed on them, and saith unto them, Receive ye the Holy Ghost" (John 20:22)

Lord Jesus Christ breathed on His disciples the Holy Spirit and they all alike received the Holy Spirit. This was done during the period of forty days of the Lord appearing to His disciples and also to many on this earth before His ascension into heaven.

It should be carefully noted that even though He breathed Holy Spirit on them He did not authorize them to go out of Jerusalem to preach the Gospel of Jesus Christ until the power came from high on.

"But ye shall receive power, after that the Holy Ghost is come upon you: and ye shall be witnesses unto me both in Jerusalem, and in all Judaea, and in Samaria, and unto the uttermost part of the earth". (Acts 1:8)

After John 20:22 some more events followed but none of the disciples went for preaching the Gospel until after Holy Spirit came upon them and they received the power.

Acts Chapter 1 commences with Luke the writer of Gospel of Luke and Acts of Apostles addresses Theophilus who was in high position in Government. The name "Theophilus" means he was a 'friend of God' that is to say he was a very pious man. However, when Luke was addressing him in Acts 1 he did not include the phrase "most excellent" which means as the time passed Theophilus was no more in Government service. Luke continues to write of all that Jesus began to do and teach in compliance to the treaty he made with him.

"It seemed good to me also, having had perfect understanding of all things from the very first, to write unto thee in order, most excellent Theophilus" (Luke 1:3)

"The former treatise have I made, O Theophilus, of all that Jesus began both to do and teach" (Acts 1:1)

The former treatise have I made, O Theophilus, of all that Jesus began both to do and teach, Until the day in which he was taken up, after that he through the Holy Ghost had given commandments unto the apostles whom he had chosen: To whom also he shewed himself alive after his passion by many infallible proofs, being seen of them forty days, and speaking of the things pertaining to the kingdom of God: And, being assembled together with them, commanded them that they should not depart from Jerusalem, but wait for the promise of the Father, which, saith he, ye have heard of me. (Acts 1:1-4)

Luke records the words of Lord Jesus Christ, who opened the understanding of His disciples that they might understand the scriptures. It is evident from this point that God only can open our understanding of the Scriptures, and until He opens our understanding we will keep groping in darkness with partial understanding, which causes us to have strife, dissensions and divisions misinterpreting scriptures.

"Then opened he their understanding, that they might understand the scriptures, And said unto them, Thus it is written, and thus it behoved Christ to suffer, and to rise from the dead the third day: And that repentance and remission of sins should be preached in his name among all nations, beginning at Jerusalem. And ye are witnesses of these things. And, behold, I send the promise of my Father upon you: but tarry ye in the city of Jerusalem, until ye be endued with power from on high" (Luke 24:45-49)

The inspired scriptures recorded in Luke 24:45-49 say that Lord Jesus Christ promised His disciples that He will send the promise of His Father upon them but that they should tarry in the city of Jerusalem, until they are endued with power from on high.

Apostle John records Lord Jesus Christ's words that the Lord spoke to the disciples of Jesus that the Comforter, who is the Holy Spirit, whom the Father will send in His name, shall teach them all things, and bring all things to their remembrance whatsoever He spoke to them.

The Lord gave them peace not as the world gives but He gave His peace. He continued saying that He is the true vine and His Father is the husbandman. Every branch in Him which bears not the fruit will be put out from the responsibility of working for Him, and the Lord purges every branch that bears fruit in order that the fruit-bearing branch may bear more fruit. Here clearly the reference is of those who are obedient to His word and work for Him, as His instruments in His hands, to proclaim the Gospel of Jesus Christ. (cf. John 14:25-31; John 15:1-2)

It was that reason why Lord Jesus Christ commanded His disciples to be at Jerusalem until the Father sends Holy Spirit to be with them forever and ever. Indeed Holy Spirit is omniscient and yet we say He came, and indwelt us for better understanding.

In the Old Testament period Holy Spirit came upon certain men and prophets and after the purpose for which He came was fulfilled He left them and went back to the Father. In the New Testament period, as the Lord promised, the Holy Spirit, the Promise of the Father came into this world on the fiftieth day after the resurrection of Lord Jesus Christ.

Therefore, there is nothing wrong in saying that He came and remained with us forever and He will leave when the Lord comes again. There will come a time when Holy Spirit will leave this world when His work is fulfilled, but until such time He leaves this earth He remains indwelling the believers in the Lord to guide them, convict them of what is right and what is not, and comforting them and never leaving them as orphans.

Holy Spirit came into this world when the Pentecost (fiftieth day) was fully come in; never to leave or re-enter time and again. It is *the* historical event and it happened once; never will be repeated. Therefore, a believer need not wait for Holy Spirit. It is the act of God. There is no such phrase as "Baptism of Holy Spirit" in the Bible. All that the said phrase means, when used as such, is that the believer in Christ is unified not only with Christ but also with other believers in the body of Christ by the work of the Spirit of God at the time of salvation of a sinner.

"For by one Spirit are we all baptized into one body, whether we be Jews or Gentiles, whether we be bond or free; and have been all made to drink into one Spirit" (1 Corinthians 12:13)

Before His crucifixion Lord Jesus Christ prayed for His glorification, and for His disciples, and also for those who receive the Lord as Savior.

"Neither pray I for these alone, but for them also which shall believe on me through their word; That they all may be one; as thou, Father, art in me, and I in thee, that they also may be one in us: that the world may believe that thou hast sent me". (John 17:20-21)

As it is recorded in Acts 1:8 the Lord said to them that they will receive power, after the Holy Spirit is come upon them, and then they will be witnesses unto Him first in Jerusalem, and then in Judaea, and in Samaria, and then unto the uttermost part of the earth. After He spoke to them He was taken up and a cloud received Him out of their sight (cf. Acts 1:8-9)

It is then the events selecting the twelfth disciple followed and then the events recorded in Acts Chapter2:2-4

It may very clearly be noted that the events that followed in Acts 2:2-4 were never repeated in History. Every word recorded in Acts 2:2-4 is very important to note.

"And suddenly there came a sound from heaven as of a rushing mighty wind, and it filled all the house where they were sitting. And there appeared unto them cloven tongues like as of fire, and it sat upon each of them. And they were all filled with the Holy Ghost, and began to speak with other tongues, as the Spirit gave them utterance" (Acts 2:2-4)

The belief that Holy Spirit comes second time or third time or many more times with rushing mighty wind, or anyone could speak the tongues the way the disciples of Jesus Christ spoke during the first occurrence of Holy Spirit coming upon them while they waited in Jerusalem, is a myth. The strange part of this is that those who believe this myth accuse others that they do not possess Holy Spirit.

CHAPTER 21
THE TWO CATEGORIES OF PEOPLE

"And it shall come to pass in the last days, saith God, I will pour out of my Spirit upon all flesh: and your sons and your daughters shall prophesy, and your young men shall see visions, and your old men shall dream dreams: And on my servants and on my handmaidens I will pour out in those days of my Spirit; and they shall prophesy: And I will shew wonders in heaven above, and signs in the earth beneath; blood, and fire, and vapour of smoke: The sun shall be turned into darkness, and the moon into blood, before that great and notable day of the Lord come: And it shall come to pass, that whosoever shall call on the name of the Lord shall be saved" (Acts 2:17-21)

As the Holy Spirit came upon the disciples, who were waiting at Jerusalem in obedience to the command from Lord Jesus, there were two kinds of people witnessing the events. The first category of people were those who believed Jesus as Messiah or mixed Gentiles from other nations who were at Jerusalem either for worshipping God or for transacting business during the feast time.

They were amazed when they saw the disciples speak in tongues, and marveled saying one to another if those who spoke tongues/languages were not from Galilee? They knew that men from Galilee were illiterates and lived a village-style of life.

When those people referred to as the men of Galilee, it was not with respect that they used the word, "Galileans"; but it was used with contempt. They wondered if those men were not from Galilee who spoke languages that every one of them understood in his/her language.

While the disciples spoke in tongues/languages, they all heard in their own languages. It was rather similar to the translated version that the parliamentarians or other members listen in their own languages when someone in an unknown or foreign language speaks from the stage in Parliament or Senate, or UN.

These who heard the disciples speak in tongues were from various regions around Jerusalem, who were in Jerusalem during the feast time. They were either pure Jews or mixed generation who in disobedience to the command from the LORD from King Solomon's time period mixed up with Gentiles. There was also Gentile Roman Government with Herod and Pilate at the helm of affairs in Israel during that period.

"And there were dwelling at Jerusalem Jews, devout men, out of every nation under heaven. Now when this was noised abroad, the multitude came together, and were confounded, because that every man heard them speak in his own language. And they were all amazed and marvelled, saying one to another, Behold, are not all these which speak Galilaeans? And how hear we every man in our own tongue, wherein we were born? Parthians, and Medes, and Elamites, and the dwellers in Mesopotamia, and in Judaea, and Cappadocia, in Pontus, and Asia, Phrygia, and Pamphylia, in Egypt, and in the parts of Libya about Cyrene, and strangers of Rome, Jews and proselytes, Cretes and Arabians, we do hear them speak in our tongues the wonderful works of God. And they were all amazed, and were in doubt, saying one to another, What meaneth this?" (Acts 2:5-12)

There was a second category of people, who were stubborn, disobedient unyielding type of people. It is not that they did not understand the language that Peter spoke; but in their rebellion they mocked at them. This is what they did to Lord Jesus also, and they are none but Jews and Gentiles who crucified Jesus on the cross. They mocked the disciples and said that those men were drunk and were of full of wine.

"Others mocking said, These men are full of new wine" (Acts 2:13)

Then Peter stood along with the other disciples, the number of whom, including Mathias was twelve. Mathias was numbered as the twelfth apostle as a consequence of Judas Iscariot betraying Jesus and subsequently committing suicide.

Peter, who took initiative to speak to the rebellious group, said that the disciples were not drunk but they spoke in fulfillment as prophesied by Joel the prophet. The prophecy of Joel says that the LORD will pour out His spirit upon all the flesh in the last days and their sons and daughters will prophecy, their young men shall see visions, and old men shall dream dreams, and on His servants on His handmaidens He will pour out in those days His Spirit, and they shall prophesy. The LORD will show wonders in heaven above, and signs in the earth. He will show blood, fire, and vapor of smoke. "The sun shall be turned into darkness and the moon into blood before that great and notable day of the Lord" comes and that whoever calls upon the name of the LORD shall be saved (cf. Acts 2:14-21; Joel 2:28-32)

"And it shall come to pass afterward, that I will pour out my spirit upon all flesh; and your sons and your daughters shall prophesy, your old men shall dream dreams, your young men shall see visions: And also upon the servants and upon the

handmaids in those days will I pour out my spirit. And I will shew wonders in the heavens and in the earth, blood, and fire, and pillars of smoke. The sun shall be turned into darkness, and the moon into blood, before the great and the terrible day of the LORD come. And it shall come to pass, that whosoever shall call on the name of the LORD shall be delivered: for in mount Zion and in Jerusalem shall be deliverance, as the LORD hath said, and in the remnant whom the LORD shall call". (Joel 2:28-32)

Notice the last few words of Joel the prophet. They are..." And it shall come to pass, that whosoever shall call on the name of the LORD shall be delivered: for in mount Zion and in Jerusalem shall be deliverance, as the LORD hath said, and in the remnant whom the LORD shall call" (Joel 2:32). Peter did not quote these words. And those last few words have much significance. That is to say the deliverance will be in "mount Zion and in Jerusalem, and in the remnant whom the LORD shall call".

It is obvious from this passage in Joel that it was addressed to Jews, who were rebellious and did not accept Lord Jesus as their Messiah. This passage clearly refers to the "Great Tribulation" period when the left-behind Jews will call upon the LORD to save them and the LORD will answer their prayer and saves them. The prophecy in Joel 2:28-32 was in two parts and only one part was fulfilled at the time when Peter spoke and other part will be fulfilled during "Great Tribulation" period.

"For the promise is unto you, and to your children, and to all that are afar off, even as many as the Lord our God shall call" (Acts 2:39)

Therefore, it is quite evident that Joel's prophecy was not fulfilled in its entirety at the time when Peter spoke those words as recorded in Acts 2: 14-27, but this prophecy will be fulfilled when it is time for God to turn the Sun into darkness, the moon into blood, and when the LORD will show blood, fire and pillars of smoke to the rebellious men left behind on this earth after the church is caught up into clouds where they meet Lord Jesus Christ.

There are related prophecies that are in connotation with Joel 2:25-32. There is a tendency to read only few verses from Joel and conclude that the days when Peter proclaimed the Gospel of Jesus Christ he was saying that those were the last days. However, if we carefully read the whole context where these verses appear it is about the restoration of nation of Israel, and of Jews, and the wrath of God that will be poured upon the heathen during those days.

The prophecy says the LORD will restore to them the yeas that the locust has eaten, the cankerworm, and cater pillar and the palmerworm that He sent among them; but now in the last days they will eat plenty and be satisfied and praise the name of the LORD their God. They will remember the LORD's promises and how He dealt with them wondrously. They shall never be ashamed. It is this period when the LORD will pour out His spirit upon all flesh.

The Psalmist prophesied that He will pour out wrath upon heathen who have not known the LORD and upon the kingdoms that have not called upon His name. It is at this time the LORD will bring the third part through the fire, and will refine His people, the children of Israel, as silver and gold are refined and tried. They will call upon the LORD's name and He will hear them. The LORD will then acknowledge them as His people and they will say that the LORD is their God. (cf. Psalm 79:6, Zechariah 13:9; Joel 2:25-32)

The miracles that the people witnessed in Peter's days soon after the Holy Spirit came upon them on the day of Pentecost were the shadow of the things that will be fulfilled in the very last days when the sun will be darkened. It is obvious that the sun was not darkened, and moon did not turn into blood during when Peter spoke as written in Acts 2:20-21)

They mocked the disciples, who spoke tongues, which were understood in their own languages, by the people of other nations who were in Jerusalem. It is they who insulted the disciples that they were drunk, and It is to them that address was made by Peter.

In his speech to the rebellious group Peter spoke in detail about Lord Jesus Christ and His crucifixion, and when they heard his speech, they were pricked in their heart and said to Peter and to the rest of the apostles, as to what they should do to be saved. In answer to their request Peter said to them to repent and be baptized and that they will receive the Holy Spirit. Peter did never say that they have to wait for the Holy Spirit to come upon them or indwell them, but he said...

"...Repent, and be baptized every one of you in the name of Jesus Christ for the remission of sins, and ye shall receive the gift of the Holy Ghost" Acts 2:38

Therefore, it is quite evident that Holy Spirit will come upon immediately and indwell any believer who was a sinner and repented of his sins and accepted Jesus Christ as his savior. This does not mean that a believer does not need subsequent fillings of the Holy Spirit. It is essential for a Christian to be filled of the Holy Spirit repeatedly in order to grow in the knowledge of the Truth and work for the Lord, but for salvation no one needs to wait for the Holy Spirit to come upon him/her. It is God's act and He will send the Holy Spirit to unite the believer with Lord Jesus Christ and also with other believers. It is also very essential to bear in mind that the very nature of Holy Spirit is a great mystery. (cf. 1 Corinthians 12:13)

Now when they heard this, they were pricked in their heart, and said unto Peter and to the rest of the apostles, Men and brethren, what shall we do? Then Peter said unto them, Repent, and be baptized every one of you in the name of Jesus Christ for the remission of sins, and ye shall receive the gift of the Holy Ghost. For the promise is unto you, and to your children, and to all that are afar off, even as many as the Lord our God shall call. And with many other words did he testify and exhort, saying, Save yourselves from this untoward generation. Then they that gladly received his word were baptized: and the same day there were added unto them about three thousand souls. (Acts 2:37-41)

It can be seen that in the Old Testament period God was concerned only about the children of Israel. Whenever there was a reference made of the nations, it was when the children of Israel defeated them or when the LORD gave instructions to the children of Israel that they should not follow the worship-pattern, idols, graven images, and/or any image made in the likeness of any creation; and norms of the heathen nations.

The LORD's undying love for the children of Israel was seen throughout the Old Testament. Even though the LORD chastised them several times, He said He loves them and will gather them as one nation finally. Lord Jesus Christ will rule whole universe and all the nations for a period of thousand years. The Church will be with Him during that period and the believers who will be with Him during those days will be Kings and priests.

Prophet Hosea's marriage with Gomer the prostitute, and her dishonesty toward Hosea and the continued love of the prophet toward her is a great spiritual example of God loving the children of Israel who were dishonest to the LORD and behaved like prostitute before Him.

And it shall come to pass afterward, that I will pour out my spirit upon all flesh; and your sons and your daughters shall prophesy, your old men shall dream dreams, your young men shall see visions: And also upon the servants and upon the handmaids in those days will I pour out my spirit. And I will shew wonders in the heavens and in the earth, blood, and fire, and pillars of smoke. The sun shall be turned into darkness, and the moon into blood, before the great and the terrible day of the LORD come. And it shall come to pass, that whosoever shall call on the name of the LORD shall be delivered: for in mount Zion and in Jerusalem shall be deliverance, as the LORD hath said, and in the remnant whom the LORD shall call. (Joel 2:28-32)

CHAPTER 22
THE GREAT GULF

Lord Jesus revealed to us a great mystery about our future life. According to His revelation, as found in Luke 16:19-13, our life does not end with our physical death, but it continues to exist in spiritual form with glorified body. Our physical is body made of dust and, therefore, it returns to dust at its lifespan appointed by God. That is not the end of life, but the life enters a different phase, which is eternal.

The soul is the principle of life consisting of our feelings, thoughts, and actions. It is the actual part of our inner man. The spirit is the breath of God. When God breathed His breath of life into the nostrils, man became a living soul.

"And the LORD God formed man of the dust of the ground, and breathed into his nostrils the breath of life; and man became a living soul" (Genesis 2:7)

THE SOUL

The soul, which is the actual part actuating inner man, continues to live, our breath returns to when we leave this earth. The death is not the cessation of life, but separation of life from the physical body. Until God gives the spiritual body an immortal glorified body the soul rests at the place appointed by God.

The body that we acquire to be with the Lord in eternity will be a glorified body, which the Lord gives us when He comes again. While we wait to receive immortal body, the soul is conscientious, able to recognize other bodies. Yet, those bodies would not be as active as our physical bodies are that we have now with soul and spirit bound within our physical body. Those bodies get activated into full life as quickly as the twinkling of an eye, when the Lord returns. The soul and spirit are controlling our thoughts and actions and the actions of our bodies depending upon how our brain yields to the encouragement, enthusiasm, or despair, temptations etc.

Now on this earth, when some thoughts come into our mind, we either yield to those thoughts or reject them. The thoughts take us in the directions we yield to them; they would be either to lead a pious life in the path of God, or in the evil way the bad thoughts to which we yield. We are capable of making decisions either to obey or to disobey such thoughts.

Without yielding to the thoughts of the mind, our bodies will remain in static condition that does not produce result. Our thoughts are guiding factors and our decision to yield to those thoughts is the cause of ether our actions leading to good or bad.

However, man is so depraved that no one can be perfect in life. Everyone yields to bad thoughts once or several times in one's life. Unless we accept or reject the thoughts of our minds we remain where we are.

THE LIGHT OF THE WORLD

Lord Jesus said...

"...I am the light of the world: he that followeth me shall not walk in darkness, but shall have the light of life" (John 8:12)

That is the reason why the Bible says when the "light" came into the world the darkness knew it not. John the Baptist came into the world, as a "lamp" lit by God, as forerunner of Lord Jesus Christ, who is the real "light". He pointed to the Lord and recognized Him as the "Lamb of God".

The sinful world did not recognize that Jesus is the Lord, and there is no salvation except by Him. In spite of Jesus doing good for men, healing them from their sickness, providing them food when they needed it, showing the way to heaven, the world crucified Him,

"And the light shineth in darkness; and the darkness comprehended it not. There was a man sent from God, whose name was John. The same came for a witness, to bear witness of the Light, that all men through him might believe" (John 1:5-7)

"While ye have light, believe in the light, that ye may be the children of light. These things spake Jesus, and departed, and did hide himself from them". (John 12:36)

The Lord's desire is that none should perish, but everyone may have life everlasting. If life was to experience annihilation then it would have been fine but it is not so. The life continues to be in either in a place of happiness or in a place of torment.

There is a misunderstanding among many of us that once a person dies, his existence is fully ceases. Of course, man's intelligence and science would say it true, but God does not say so. God says we will pay for what we have done on this earth.

LAMB OF GOD

"The next day John seeth Jesus coming unto him, and saith, Behold the Lamb of God, which taketh away the sin of the world. (John 1:29)

"And looking upon Jesus as he walked, he saith, Behold the Lamb of God!" (John 1:36).

Lord Jesus is the incarnate God, who came into this world in the form of servant and in the likeness of man leaving behind the entire glory that He had with the Father. He lived among men, and offered Himself as substitutionary sacrifice on behalf of all of us in order that we may accept Him as Lord and Savior, and believe that God raised Him from the dead. Those who believe in Him will not perish but will have everlasting life.

THE HISTORY

Here is the real history of a rich man and a poor man named "Lazarus" revealed by Lord Jesus Christ to us in order that we may be cautious and know the reality. Inasmuch as the Lord pointedly shown a man by his name, it is obvious that it was not a parable. In none of the parables Jesus identified a man by his name.

Lord Jesus said there was a rich man, who enjoyed the worldly pleasures. He had purple and fine linen to wear on this earth. There was also another man, who was poor, and his name was "Lazarus". While the rich man enjoyed worldly pleasure and ate sumptuously every day, the poor man "Lazarus", full or sores, lived at his gate, desiring to eat the crumbs that fell from the rich man's table. In addition, dogs came and licked his sores.

The time hit both of them, and as death was inevitable, both died at their appointed time, which is known only to sovereign God. Our time is also appointed by God and we cannot fight against the LORD's desire nor can we resist it to say alive here to enjoy the pleasures of this world forever.

It is very common to say that while we have one life, live it pleasing to body and mind; but hardly does one who says so knows that everyone has to give an account of all that one has done on this earth, and reap consequences eternally.

Lazarus, the beggar died and was carried by angels into the bosom of Abraham. The rich man also died and was buried. The rich man saw from the hell he is in the beggar, Lazarus in Abraham's bosom, at a great distance. There was a great gulf between them, and yet they could communicate with each other, and were conscientious. While the rich man was suffering torment, Lazarus was being comforted and joyful in Abraham's bosom. The rich man lifted his eyes and saw Lazarus in Abraham's bosom and begged for a drop of water with the finger of Lazarus that he may cool his tongue. The rich man said "I am tormented in this flame". The two souls mentioned here, besides Abraham's soul, were conscientious and lived quite a great deal apart in two different locations.

Abraham replied to the soul of rich man to look back to his life on earth, and remember how he received the good things and Lazarus bad things at the gate of rich man's house. Now in their conscientious state in different places; one of joyful bosom of Abraham, and the other in a place where he is tormented have their rewards of one being blessed and the other being tormented. The rich man anxiously craved for a drop of water from the finger of Lazarus.

Even if Abraham had desire of sending Lazarus to the rich man with water, he would not be able to reach the rich man in a place of torment because God created such a great gulf between these two places that none can pass from one location to the other.

THE CONSEQUENCES OF REJECTION

The rich man realized that he did all the bad in his physical life on this earth and now reaping the consequences of evil doings, while Lazarus is happy enjoying rest and peace in the bosom of Abraham. The rich man had concern for his five brothers that they may not reach the place of torment where he was now, and therefore, prays to Abraham to send Lazarus to earth to preach them of the serious consequences of living evil way on this earth.

However, Abraham said to the rich man that they have Moses and the prophets to teach them and preach the good news of place of rest and peace, and joyful life in eternity. The rich man pleads with Abraham saying if Lazarus went from the dead and preached them of the good news, they would repent of their evil ways and reach the place where Lazarus was. Abraham's reply was that if they did not listen and pay heed to the Gospel from those who are alive on the earth, they would least pay heed to the one who went from the dead and preached t them.

SALVATION MESSAGE

While good news of Lord Jesus Christ is being preached either verbally or in writing, it is now the apt time for those who have not repented yet of their sins to repent and turn to God by confessing that Jesus is the Lord, and God raised Him from the dead. Bible says there is no salvation in any other than in Him.

If one rejects Jesus now, a time will come when one will be forced to fall down on his knees and acknowledge with his mouth that Jesus is Lord (cf. Acts 4: Philippians 2:9-10; Romans 10:9,10)

HOLY SCRIPTURES

For thou wilt not leave my soul in hell; neither wilt thou suffer thine Holy One to see corruption. (Psalms 16:10)

Jesus answered and said unto him, Verily, verily, I say unto thee, Except a man be born again, he cannot see the kingdom of God. Nicodemus saith unto him, How can a man be born when he is old? can he enter the second time into his mother's womb, and be born? Jesus answered, Verily, verily, I say unto thee, Except a man be born of water and of the Spirit, he cannot enter into the kingdom of God. That which is born of the flesh is flesh; and that which is born of the Spirit is spirit. (John 3:3-6)

For God so loved the world, that he gave his only begotten Son, that whosoever believeth in him should not perish, but have everlasting life. For God sent not his Son into the world to condemn the world; but that the world through him might be saved. (John 3:16-17)

That if thou shalt confess with thy mouth the Lord Jesus, and shalt believe in thine heart that God hath raised him from the dead, thou shalt be saved. For with the heart man believeth unto righteousness; and with the mouth confession is made unto salvation. (Romans 10:9-10)

Neither is there salvation in any other: for there is none other name under heaven given among men, whereby we must be saved. (Acts 4:12)

That at the name of Jesus every knee should bow, of things in heaven, and things in earth, and things under the earth; And that every tongue should confess that Jesus Christ is Lord, to the glory of God the Father. Wherefore, my beloved, as ye have always obeyed, not as in my presence only, but now much more in my absence, work out your own salvation with fear and trembling. (Philippians 2:10-12)

CHAPTER 23
OF THE HOLY SPIRIT

"Jesus saith unto him, I am the way, the truth, and the life: no man cometh unto the Father, but by me" (John 14:6)

Our endeavors should be to do good works instead of remaining static or do evil to others, when thoughts persuade us of any action on our part. We are not supposed to remain static in our actions, but to yield to our thoughts to do well, and increase in the knowledge of the Truth of God. Lord Jesus Christ is the way, the truth and the life.

The Bible says we are not supposed to remain like babes in the knowledge of the Truth of God, but become mature like those who could digest meat and give up milk (cf. Hebrews 15:23-14)

There is no dearth of number of people who have wrong notion that doing bad to others or even kill is God's service. They think they are pleasing their gods. The Bible warns us not to do such evil to anyone or harm anyone.

We are all created by God and when He created man He did it to make man in His own image. Alas! As a result of the first man and first woman yielding to evil, Sin entered in to the world and resulted in not only Spiritual death on the same they transgressed God's verbal law, but also suffered physical death in due course of time.

The death reigned from Adam until Moses, even though written Word of God was not there, and thereafter it continued. By the first man who was made a living soul, the Sin permeated into all of his descendants, but the by the last Adam, who was Lord Jesus Christ the righteousness is imputed to those who accept Him as Lord. The Lord was made a quickening spirit, a life-imparting spirit, and, therefore, we have our life in Him. As Jesus was raised from the dead; so will we be raised from the dead! (cf. Romans 5:12-19)

"And so it is written, The first man Adam was made a living soul; the last Adam was made a quickening spirit" (1 Corinthians 15:45)

Unless we trust God and gain His righteousness by repenting of our sins, and confessing them to Him seeking humbly of forgiveness, we cannot receive salvation.

Jesus spoke to His disciples of evil that is prevailing in the world. He warned them to be careful and watchful of the persecutions that the followers of Lord Jesus Christ would suffer. Before His crucifixion He also said to them that they would be scattered and none but the Father would be with Him when He suffers on the cross for our sake.

Lord Jesus spoke of the evil that is present in the world in order that they may have peace, the peace that He gives. He promises them that He will be with them till the end. He instructed them to be of good cheer, because He overcame the world.

The disciples believed that Lord Jesus came into this world from the Father. God is love and He loved us first, and that is the reason why He sent His only Son into this world, in order that we might believe in Him and receive everlasting life. The Father loves the followers of Lord Jesus Christ.

While the disciples of Lord Jesus Christ were pondering on the discourse the Lord had with them, the Lord tells them that unless He goes to the Father, the Comforter will not into this world. It is essential that as per the plan of the Father, He should go to the Father. As they were not sure of what the Lord was speaking of His going to the Father, the Lord explains to them that after He goes to the Father, He would send the Holy Spirit, who is the Comforter, who will be with them to guide them in every step of their ways. The Holy Spirit, who is the Comforter, "will reprove the world of sin, and of righteousness, and of judgment".

If Christians are left without the help of the Holy Spirit, they would stumble from their faith an fall to perish. Holy Spirit, therefore, continuously helps Christians to be in the path of righteousness. He will guide Christians to keep aloof from apostasy.

The persecutors think that they are doing God's service when they put Christians out from the Churches and kill them. They do so because they have not known the love of the Father, and of the Son Lord Jesus Christ.

One of the Ten Commandments is "Thou shalt not kill" (Exodus 20:13) and Lord Jesus Christ condenses all the commands into two simple commandments, and they are:

"Jesus said unto him, Thou shalt love the Lord thy God with all thy heart, and with all thy soul, and with all thy mind. This is the first and great commandment. And the second is like unto it, Thou shalt love thy neighbour as thyself. On these two commandments hang all the law and the prophets" (Matthew 22:37-40)

Sin is the transgression of the Law. God's command is that we should love God with all our heart, with all our soul, and with our entire mind. That is the first command, and the second is that we should love our neighbor as ourselves. All the commandments are condensed into these two commandments.

The first thing the Holy Spirit will do is to judge the world of Sin. The violation of Law, which results in Sin, is the cause of all evil in this world. The Lord says He will go to the Father, and they will see Him no more. Therefore, it is essential that they should have Holy Spirit in them. The Lord was righteous and innocent, and yet Jews and Gentiles together crucified Him on the cross.

In such circumstances as we face in this world, of persecution, the Holy Spirit will help us and guide us with His peace. The Bible says...

"Blessed are they which are persecuted for righteousness' sake: for theirs is the kingdom of heaven" (Matthew 5:10)

The prince of this world is Satan, who was defeated at the cross, when it pleased the Father to bruise His Son on the cross on for our sake.

Lord Jesus, who knew no sin, became sin for our and bore our sin on Him, in order that we may receive redemption from sin by believing in His atoning sacrifice on the Cross. He became our mediator, and He is our High Priest, Prophet and King. He is the King of kings, Lord of lords, and the God of gods.

(Ref: John 16:1-33; II Cor. 5:21)

CHAPTER 24
DO NOT BE UNEQUALLY YOKED

"Be ye not unequally yoked together with unbelievers: for what fellowship hath righteousness with unrighteousness? and what communion hath light with darkness? And what concord hath Christ with Belial? or what part hath he that believeth with an infidel? And what agreement hath the temple of God with idols? for ye are the temple of the living God; as God hath said, I will dwell in them, and walk in them; and I will be their God, and they shall be my people. Wherefore come out from among them, and be ye separate, saith the Lord, and touch not the unclean thing; and I will receive you, And will be a Father unto you, and ye shall be my sons and daughters, saith the Lord Almighty" (2 Corinthians 6:14-18)

When the true light came into this world the darkness comprehended it not, rather it continued to engulf mankind into yielding to the worldly activities. The darkness perverted the truth and projected falsehood and sin among men as pleasing, delightful and acceptable to man.

Man, who yielded to the temptation of the devil in the Garden of Eden, continues to fall into the devouring mouth of Satan. Unless he takes refuge in the light and in the truth he will perish in his sin and face eternal damnation. Falsehood and sin never prevail and will never bring happiness to man. Sin never brings lasting happiness in the lives of men. It is transient, temporal.

God has been warning and chastening man from the time he fell into sin in the Garden of Eden, and yet very few come into the light to enjoy the true pleasantness. The true pleasantness, joy, happiness, rest, and everlasting life are available in the only Son of God, who is our Lord Jesus Christ. He gave His life for our sake in order that we may by accepting Him as savior have light in our lives and everlasting life to be with the Lord forever and ever.

Christ, who is savior, has no concord with the devil, which is darkness that never can provide salvation. The only one who can rescue us from the bondage of slavery under sin is Lord Jesus Christ. He is the Son of God, and very God Himself, who incarnated and came into the world in the likeness of man to die for us. His action did not end with His sacrifice, but he came out alive with glorified body. His body did not see corruption in the grave. He was raised by God on the third day after His death.

The death did not have victory over Him; rather He defeated Satan on the cross. He had victory over death. Inasmuch as He was triumphant over death, we who die in Christ will also live like Him and in Him surely after our death, which in the case of believer is not cessation of life, but mere sleep. The soul , which is our inner man, never sleeps but will be under the care of God in a place designated by Him. Until the Lord returns with the angels and the believers who have already gone before us to Him our souls will be conscientious in paradise with the Lord. Our physical bodies which are made of dust will return to dust, but on resurrection we will have glorified bodies. The dead in Christ will rise first and the live ones will follow them in that order (ref. 1 Thessalonians 4:16,17)

Believer's life is a separated life from that of unbeliever and that separation never unites to last long. That is why according to scriptures a believer should never marry an unbeliever. That worldly union will never last but surely breaks apart one day or the other. God and Satan cannot unite and never can exist together.

Either one has to be under the slavery under Satan, or have perfect rest and joyful and eternal life with eternal God. Righteousness and unrighteousness can never go together just as it is true that light and darkness cannot exist together. Even when a small speck of light entering darkroom dispels darkness and the darkness instantly flees. God has provided light for us, and that light is our Lord Jesus Christ. It is for man to take refuge in the Lord and dispel darkness from our lives.

After accepting Lord Jesus Christ as our savior, our soul is instantly saved with indwelling of Holy Spirit, who is the earnest for our salvation. It is guaranteed relief from sin and provision of everlasting life with the Lord. None can take us from the hands of our God and no harm can come upon us. Believe in the one who can kill body and soul, rather than man who can utmost kill the body but not the soul of any man. None can do any harm to saved soul. We will receive glorified bodies compatible to be with the Lord in heaven.

"Now he which stablisheth us with you in Christ, and hath anointed us, is God; Who hath also sealed us, and given the earnest of the Spirit in our hearts" (2 Corinthians 1:21-22)

"In whom ye also trusted, after that ye heard the word of truth, the gospel of your salvation: in whom also after that ye believed, ye were sealed with that holy Spirit of promise, Which is the earnest of our inheritance until the redemption of the purchased possession, unto the praise of his glory" (Ephesians 1:13-14)

It is, therefore, imperative that a believer should never be yoked with unbeliever in marriage. This does not preclude man's daily interactions with unbeliever. God's instructions for our blessed future life is that we by being yoked to the believer will be with Him.

When Holy Spirit is in our hearts our body is the temple of God, because God lives in that temple. God's instructions are that we should not defile our holy temple by allowing evil to enter into our hearts and we should not commit sin.

Earlier, in his first epistle (1 Corinthians 6:15-20) Paul wrote that our bodies are the members of Christ, and He questions there as to how dare we should be to share the members of our body with harlot? He wishes that God may forbid such union. He asserts the fact that he who joins his members of his body with harlot becomes one with her.

The scripture from Genesis is clear about marriage that man shall leave his father and mother and shall cleave to his wife, and they will be one flesh (cf. Genesis 2:24). If so, how a believer can allow the members of his body to be shared by harlot? We can never unite the Lord's body with that of harlot. So, is the case of unholy union of believer with unbeliever in marriage!

Lord Jesus Christ has absolutely no part with Satan; nor does He have any part with an infidel. There can be absolutely no agreement between the body of a believer, which is the temple of God and where Holy Spirit dwells, and with that of the temples of idols.

God says He will dwell in the bodies of believers, and walk in them, and He will be the God of them, and they shall be His people. Therefore, He commands us to be separate, not be unequally yoked with worldly things and with unbelievers. If we obey and follow His commands, the Lord God Almighty assures that He will be our God and we shall be His sons, and daughters.

CHAPTER 25
RIGHTEOUSNESS OF GOD

"For he hath made him to be sin for us, who knew no sin; that we might be made the righteousness of God in him". (2 Corinthians 5:21)

Theology can sometimes be bizarre when someone puts his knowledge makes wrong interpretation of the Scriptures rather than depending on what the Scripture says. Bible says "...that no prophecy of the scripture is of any private interpretation" (cf. 2 Peter 1:20). Prophecy here is within the purview of the testimony of Jesus as the scripture says in Revelation 19:10b.

One such wrong interpretation is that one has to believe in the perfect obedience by Jesus to the Father while He was on this earth. While it is true that Jesus lived in perfect obedience to the Father, it cannot be made as conditional necessity to receive salvation, inasmuch as there is no scripture to support this phenomenon. They call this as "active obedience of Jesus" and they believe that it is mandatory to believe in such "active obedience of Jesus to have imputation of righteousness.

There are varied interpretations as to how salvation is achieved. While the Bible is clear that salvation is by grace through faith, some say the efficacy of the blood of Lord Jesus Christ shed on the cross was not enough to be saved, but a man has to live by the law to receive righteousness. They even have gone to the extent of naming the obedience of Jesus Christ into two categories.

TWO CATEGORIES OF OBEDIENCE?

There is no scripture that demands to name the obedience of Jesus to the Father into two categories. The two categories of obedience of Jesus, according to them are:

1. Active Obedience of Jesus
2. Passive obedience of Jesus

It seems good to study these two aspects of obedience; but imposing a condition that belief in both these two categories as mandatory for receiving salvation is utterly a false teaching. According to them the active obedience of Jesus is recognized by the implicit obedience to the Father, of Jesus Christ before His death on the cross. The passive obedience of Jesus, according to them is recognized by the implicit obedience of Jesus to the Father in yielding Himself for crucifixion.

THE SON OF GOD

The testimony of Lord Jesus Christ is that He is the Son of God. In order for to be reconciled to God for the trespass Adam had committed, God sent His only begotten Son into this world that whosoever believes in Him shall not perish but have everlasting life. The Son was born of the Virgin Mary when Holy Spirit came upon her and the power of the Highest overshadowed her. The Holy thing that was born of her was called the "Son of God" (cf. Luke 1:35; Matt.1:23).

HE WAS MADE LITTLE LOWER THAN ANGELS

The transgression of God's command that Adam had committed, was imputed to him as sin, which was inherited by all mankind. That sin had to be fully paid for and the only one qualified to pay for the sins of mankind was Lord Jesus Christ (cf. Hebrews 2:9).

Lord Jesus took the position little lower than angels and came into this world in the form of servant and in the likeness of man. It was necessary for Him to take such position to qualify Himself to taste the substitutionary death on behalf of sinners, and it pleased the Father to bruise Him on the cross. He was obedient unto death, even unto death by crucifixion. The Bible says that there is remission of sins unless blood is shed.

SUBSTITUTIONARY DEATH

In the Old Testament it was seen how animals were used as sacrifice as substitutionary death to cover the sin of man, who offers such sacrifice and confesses his sin. It was not a permanent solution until Lord Jesus Christ shed His precious blood upon the cross for the remission of our sins. He died substitutionary death on behalf of us fulfilling all the law of the Old Testament.

Lord Jesus came to fulfill the law and He did it by his birth as the holy one born of the virgin Mary and by living a holy life and offering Himself as a sacrifice on behalf of us in due time. It was in due time that He came into this world in flesh. (cf. Romans 5:6; John 1:1-14)

He was Holy in the form of God before the foundations of the world and thought it not robbery to be equal with the Father but gave up His glory and made Himself of no reputation when He came into this world.

Lord Jesus, who was the incarnate God, He lived among men and was obedient to the Father. He had the power to forgive sins of sinner.

"But that ye may know that the Son of man hath power on earth to forgive sins, (then saith he to the sick of the palsy,) Arise, take up thy bed, and go unto thine house" (Matthew 9:6)

He saw how terrible it was to take upon Himself the sin of man to redeem from the bondage of slavery under sin, and yet He was of the desire to fulfill the will of the Father (cf. Phil. 2:5-10; Matt. 26:42). He was Holy, and His Holy and He will be holy.

It was not by His obedience to the Father that He qualified to be called Holy and sinless, but being God Himself even before He came into the world, and being born in the womb of Virgin Mary He was Holy and sinless. There was no union of Joseph and Mary before Jesus was born in the womb of Virgin Mary "for that which is conceived in her is of the Holy Ghost" (Matt. 1:20b)

THE LAST ADAM

We, human beings are not born with Holiness such as Lord Jesus was born, but we are made of dust. By one man's sin we are all made sinners and by one man's obedience we have the privilege to claim righteousness. One man who was disobedient to God's command was Adam, but by the obedience of one, who came into this world as man, was the Jesus, who was also called as the "last Adam"

"And so it is written, The first man Adam was made a living soul; the last Adam was made a quickening spirit" (1 Corinthians 15:45)

"For as by one man's disobedience many were made sinners, so by the obedience of one shall many be made righteous" (Romans 5:19)

DID CHRIST DIE IN VAIN?

Apostle Paul writes...

"I do not frustrate the grace of God: for if righteousness come by the law, then Christ is dead in vain" (Galatians 2:21)

"O foolish Galatians, who hath bewitched you, that ye should not obey the truth, before whose eyes Jesus Christ hath been evidently set forth, crucified among you?" (Galatians 3:1)

Paul continues to write that Abraham believed God and his belief in God it was accounted to him for righteousness. Therefore those who are of faith are all the children of Abraham. "The scripture foreseeing that God would justify the heathen through faith" this good news was preached to Abraham.

CAN MAN FULFILL ENTIRE LAW OF GOD?

No one can be justified under the law, which only points sin, but does not provide salvation. All those who claim salvation under the works of the law are under the curse, inasmuch as not a single person on the earth can keep the entire law God gave to man. No man is justified by the law in the sight of God. Man, who commits himself to abide by the works of the law for salvation and justification will live by the law and the grace of God is not available for him. Because man cannot fulfill all the law he will remain cursed. On the contrary, if man believes in the grace of God, and accepts that Christ, who was made a curse for us and has redeemed from the curse of the law, he will be saved and justified as innocent. (cf. Galatians 3:6-14)

HERESY

This is where some believe that when God forgives sin man is restored to the position of Adam before he sinned, but does not make him righteous before God. Such belief is nothing but heresy. When God declares a man sinless it is the justification and the imputation of God's righteousness to man. There is nothing more to be done by man. It is the action that God takes and it is none of man's actions. There is no scripture to show that man has to live by righteous works or be subject to the Old Testament laws to be reckoned as righteous.

"For therein is the righteousness of God revealed from faith to faith: as it is written, The just shall live by faith". (Romans 1:17)

Putting in the mouths of people that which is not there in the scriptures is like making few statements as to how would the weather be in heaven. Would be like that of the weather near Indian Ocean, or some other ocean? The scripture is clear that there would be no sea in eternity, and Lord Jesus Christ is the light in heaven. There is no Sun or Moon required there to light heaven. Disputing what is in the Bible and adding that which is not there in the Bible is in bad taste of theology.

Romans 3:21 does not justify to take a position to state that man has to believe in the active obedience of Jesus, but the meaning of the verse should be read in its context.

"But now the righteousness of God without the law is manifested, being witnessed by the law and the prophets" (Romans 3:21)

Romans 3:21 is in the midst of Romans 3:19-24.

"Now we know that what things soever the law saith, it saith to them who are under the law: that every mouth may be stopped, and all the world may become guilty before God. Therefore by the deeds of the law there shall no flesh be justified in his sight: for by the law is the knowledge of sin. But now the righteousness of God without the law is manifested, being witnessed by the law and the prophets; Even the righteousness of God which is by faith of Jesus Christ unto all and upon all them that believe: for there is no difference: For all have sinned, and come short of the glory of God; Being justified freely by his grace through the redemption that is in Christ Jesus" (Romans 3:19-24)

LOVE OF GOD

It is the righteousness of God that is imputed to man and it is by faith of Jesus Christ unto all and upon all them that believe. The leading design of the Gospel of Jesus Christ is to evince the love of God. Few scriptures in support of this fact are...

"For God so loved the world, that he gave his only begotten Son, that whosoever believeth in him should not perish, but have everlasting life". (John 3:16)

"But God, who is rich in mercy, for his great love wherewith he loved us" (Ephesians 2:4)

"Now our Lord Jesus Christ himself, and God, even our Father, which hath loved us, and hath given us everlasting consolation and good hope through grace" (2 Thessalonians 2:16)

"He that loveth not knoweth not God; for God is love" (1 John 4:8)

BY GRACE THROUGH FAITH

None of these verses or any other verse in the Bible constrains us to believe that man has to believe in the active obedience of Jesus Christ. Rather scripture acknowledges that man is not perfect and cannot keep the entire law of God. It is by grace through faith in Jesus Christ that God's righteousness is imputed instantly to the believer.

While we attempt surely to keep ourselves free from sin even after being born again, yet because we are living in this sinful world we might commit sins. Such sins are forgiven by God upon confession.

"If we say that we have no sin, we deceive ourselves, and the truth is not in us. If we confess our sins, he is faithful and just to forgive us our sins, and to cleanse us from all unrighteousness. If we say that we have not sinned, we make him a liar, and his word is not in us" (1 John 1:8-10)

Lord Jesus Christ has set us up on a very high plane to know what it means to sin and what exactly constitutes sin. He said that whoever is angry with his brother without a cause shall be in danger of judgment, and if anyone says to the other "you fool" shall be in danger of hell fire. The definition of "adultery", as Jesus said, is the lusting after woman (cf. Matt.5:22; 27-28). The Lord gave two commands, and they are...

"... Thou shalt love the Lord thy God with all thy heart, and with all thy soul, and with all thy mind. This is the first and great commandment. And the second is like unto it, Thou shalt love thy neighbour as thyself. On these two commandments hang all the law and the prophets". (Matthew 22:37-40)

Who could fulfill all these commands? If anyone were to fully keep these commands all through his life, it would be hard to call him less than god. Therefore, it is the grace that is available for us to confess our sins to Him and receive pardon. However, if we repeatedly commit sins only to avail the privilege of being forgiven, it is tantamount to being considered as not born-again in the first place. Therefore, the Scriptures say…

"He that committeth sin is of the devil; for the devil sinneth from the beginning. For this purpose the Son of God was manifested, that he might destroy the works of the devil. Whosoever is born of God doth not commit sin; for his seed remaineth in him: and he cannot sin, because he is born of God". (1 John 3:8-9)

The Lord said our righteousness should exceed the hypocrisy of Pharisees, who pay the tithe of mint and cumin and omit the weightier matters of the law, judgement, mercy and faith (cf. Matthew 23:23)

SANCTIFIED ONCE FOR ALL

Hebrews 10th Chapter has powerful text to defend that the death of Jesus Christ (which some call as "passive obedience of Jesus Christ"), was enough for man, who accepts Lordship of Jesus Christ, to be justified as righteous before God.

"Then said I, Lo, I come (in the volume of the book it is written of me,) to do thy will, O God. Above when he said, Sacrifice and offering and burnt offerings and offering for sin thou wouldest not, neither hadst pleasure therein; which are offered by the law; Then said he, Lo, I come to do thy will, O God. He taketh away the first, that he may establish the second. By the which will we are sanctified through the offering of the body of Jesus

Christ once for all. And every priest standeth daily ministering and offering oftentimes the same sacrifices, which can never take away sins" (Hebrews 10:7-11)

JESUS FULFILLED LAW FOR US

Lord Jesus Christ, of whom the Old Testament spoke of, came into the world in due time, and by His death we are sanctified once for all. He fulfilled the entire law on behalf of us, and, therefore, there is no necessity for us to keep Old Testament laws. It is enough if we keep His two commandments. If by chance we fail to keep them, there is always forgiveness upon confession and on repentance. This does not preclude man making every endeavor in his life after being born again to keep himself holy and blameless before God by obeying the two commandments that Lord Jesus gave to us.

"Now the just shall live by faith: but if any man draw back, my soul shall have no pleasure in him. But we are not of them who draw back unto perdition; but of them that believe to the saving of the soul" (Hebrews 10:38-39)

"For what the law could not do, in that it was weak through the flesh, God sending his own Son in the likeness of sinful flesh, and for sin, condemned sin in the flesh: That the righteousness of the law might be fulfilled in us, who walk not after the flesh, but after the Spirit" (Romans 8:3-4)

NO CONDEMNATION

"There is therefore now no condemnation to them which are in Christ Jesus, who walk not after the flesh, but after the Spirit" (Romans 8:1)

"Who shall separate us from the love of Christ? shall tribulation, or distress, or persecution, or famine, or nakedness, or peril, or sword?" (Romans 8:35)

"For I am persuaded, that neither death, nor life, nor angels, nor principalities, nor powers, nor things present, nor things to come, Nor height, nor depth, nor any other creature, shall be able to separate us from the love of God, which is in Christ Jesus our Lord" (Romans 8:38-39)

We are no longer slaves to sin; and because we are yoked to Christ we are set free from the penalty of being cast into the "lake of fire". The power of sin has no dominion over us.

www.ingramcontent.com/pod-product-compliance
Lightning Source LLC
Chambersburg PA
CBHW060517030426
42337CB00015B/1919